Let's Talk About Race in the Early Years

We all have biases and our biases, whether conscious or not, can prevent us from teaching and supporting children equitably. We cannot turn a blind eye to this, no matter how uncomfortable it may feel to tackle the difficult questions.

This groundbreaking book is a must-read for all early years professionals working with babies, toddlers, young children, and their families. Its practical and accessible guidance provides the tools and techniques you need to identify and confront discriminatory practices, with strategies to break down barriers and tackle these complicated issues sensitively and constructively. Reflective questions facilitate active engagement with a wealth of case studies and encourage you to evaluate your own practice. Each chapter builds your confidence and ability to create dynamic and anti-racist learning environments that embrace and celebrate difference and will ensure your setting fosters a positive sense of identity and belonging.

Let's Talk About Race in the Early Years gives practitioners the language and tools they need to create an environment where all children can shine and is essential reading for all early years professionals.

Stella Louis is a multi-award-winning freelance early years consultant, trainer, and author, working with all forms of early years settings, as well as parents, government departments and charities.

Hannah Betteridge is an experienced policy professional and public servant. In both her undergraduate and postgraduate degrees, Hannah primarily focused on uncovering the impact of race, stereotypes, and bias on outcomes for individuals from Black and Asian backgrounds in Britain.

"Every early years setting needs a copy of this book. Louis and Betteridge, two generations of the same family, share their combined research, knowledge and lived experiences generously to challenge and support practitioners and families to develop more equitable practice for young children of colour. The balance of lived examples from practice, current research data and Black contributors make this a unique book. Use this book for personal reflection, in your training or book group to guide your discussions and to effect change. We can all, 'Do something. Do more. Do better.'"

– **Jane Whinnett MBE**, Froebel Trust Travelling Tutor,
Froebel in Childhood Practice, University of Edinburgh

"I humbly recommend this book to all who want to move equality and inclusive practice forward by talking about race and encouraging all members of early years communities – children, families - to value diversity and challenge bias. This book is challenging and practical; it addresses the needs of educators, wherever they are on their personal and professional journey to break the cycle of discrimination in their settings. The authors shine a light on ways to 'identify and confront discriminatory and prejudicial practice' and at the same time they challenge readers to examine their own thinking and practice. It is – in parts – a necessarily difficult read; there is nothing easy or comfortable about racism. It is also an enabling book; offering readers tools to tackle bias, and to create honest, dynamic and anti-racist environments where all children – and their families – thrive. In the hands of committed educators, this book will make a difference."

– **Professor Dame Cathy Nutbrown**,
The School Education Faculty of Social Sciences,
The University of Sheffield

"This book challenges early childhood educators to think deeply about personal and institutional racism and to act decisively against it. It may be difficult to raise and discuss the inequities of racial prejudice in early years settings. Yet in our increasingly diverse and also increasingly polarised societies, it is crucial that early childhood educators know how to recognise, discuss and counter biases and racism in themselves, and others, including young children. The authors explain why this is so, inviting readers to join them as they share their clear perspective about race, anti-racism and ways to work towards equity and genuine inclusion. Using personal experiences and case studies, research based understandings and practical exercises, they guide the reader through a thought provoking and valuable process."

– **Carole Bloch**, Extraordinary Professor,
Language Education, University of the Western Cape

"*Let's Talk About Race in the Early Years* is *exactly* what we need right now [...]. Stella and Hannah weave in best practice throughout the book ensuring that observation of children is key, as well as developing relationships with families and including music, song and rhyme as an example of ensuring cultural relevance and providing a window into new spaces to explore [...]. The authors present clear definitions and explanations with real life and relatable case studies to ensure that all the messages make sense and can be applied to the reader's own practice. The book highlights the challenges that we need to overcome to unpick the nuance that we learn from the world and make conscious effort to be better citizens, as well as encouraging and teaching children the same."

– **Rachna Joshi**, Freelance Writer and
Early Childhood Consultant

Let's Talk About Race in the Early Years

Stella Louis and Hannah Betteridge

Routledge
Taylor & Francis Group

LONDON AND NEW YORK

Designed cover image: Stella Louis and Hannah Betteridge

First published 2024
by Routledge
4 Park Square, Milton Park, Abingdon, Oxon OX14 4RN

and by Routledge
605 Third Avenue, New York, NY 10158

Routledge is an imprint of the Taylor & Francis Group, an informa business

British Library Cataloguing-in-Publication Data
A catalogue record for this book is available from the British Library

Library of Congress Cataloging-in-Publication Data
Names: Louis, Stella, author. | Betteridge, Hannah, author.
Title: Let's talk about race in the early years / Stella Louis and Hannah
Betteridge.
Description: Abingdon, Oxon; New York, NY: Routledge, 2024. |
Includes bibliographical references and index. |
Identifiers: LCCN 2023059248 (print) | LCCN 2023059249 (ebook) |
ISBN 9781032169606 (hardback) | ISBN 9781032169620 (paperback) |
ISBN 9781003251149 (ebook)
Subjects: LCSH: Early childhood education–Social aspects. |
Racism in education–Prevention.
Classification: LCC LB1139.23 .L68 2024 (print) | LCC LB1139.23 (ebook) |
DDC 372.21–dc23/eng/20240122
LC record available at https://lccn.loc.gov/2023059248
LC ebook record available at https://lccn.loc.gov/2023059249

ISBN: 978-1-032-16960-6 (hbk)
ISBN: 978-1-032-16962-0 (pbk)
ISBN: 978-1-003-25114-9 (ebk)

DOI: 10.4324/9781003251149

Typeset in Optima
by Deanta Global Publishing Services, Chennai, India

To Mary and Vincent Louis, this book would never have been written without your bravery and resilience in forging a new path in an unfamiliar and hostile land.

For Ava and my beautiful star baby, though your time in this world was fleeting, your tiny footprints left an everlasting imprint on our hearts. You made us hope for a better world; one that sees beauty in difference, where children are free to be whoever they want to be, no matter the colour of their skin. This book is for both of you.

Contents

Contents

Contributors

Professor Nathan Holder is a musician, author, and education consultant, with a particular focus on diversity and decolonisation. He has performed or recorded with artists such as Ghetts, The Arkells and Emeli Sandé, and serves on several boards, including the All Party Parliamentary Group for Africa. He is the author of several books – *I Wish I Didn't Quit: Music Lessons*, *Where Are All the Black Female Composers?* and *The World of Music*.

Liz Pemberton is the award-winning Director of The Black Nursery Manager Ltd – a training and consultancy company focusing on anti-racist practice within Early Years. With 18 years in the education sector, Liz's roles have included secondary school teacher, guest lecturer and up until 2020, Nursery Manager, allowing her to support and educate early years professionals in a variety of forums.

Foreword

Laura Henry-Allain MBE

I was honoured to receive an email from Stella and Hannah asking me to write the foreword to their new book, *Let's Talk About Race in the Early Years*. The book also includes contributions from Liz Pemberton and Nathan Holder; I admire and respect both of their work. There was no debate to be had: I said yes straight away. This groundbreaking book will change the hearts and minds of educators and have a positive impact on the children they work with for years to come.

My first qualification in Early Years, back in 1989, was the renowned NNEB certificate in Nursery Nursing. If you are an NNEB graduate, you will remember the 60 child development observations as well as the various placements that made up the course. Although the NNEB qualification was very robust in certain aspects, it lacked content on race and racism. It covered 'cultural awareness', which involved sharing information about different groups, largely with a focus on religion. At best, this was very stereotypical – for example, discussing a person from the Jewish or Islamic faith, their behaviour, and certain traits linked to their religion. What we did not cover was diversity and inclusion, and more specifically, race and racism.

I have worked both in a local authority role and for Ofsted, and the view at times within local and central government was that all was well if a setting had a few resources and materials that depicted 'differences', whatever that means! A setting would get a tick in the box for meeting that particular requirement. In the days when settings had a month's notice for their inspection, they used to share the 'Black doll' with each other in some cases. This demonstrated to me at the time, and even now, that there was no reflection on the why and how a range of positive resources and materials are important for every child. For me, it is about how educators understand structural and systemic racism and how they use resources to assist children with their learning and development in racism. Positive resources and materials only benefit children if educators know why they are important and equally how they empower children.

Throughout my career in Early Years, the continuous personal and professional development that I undertook still focused more on 'cultural awareness' rather than race, especially the impact of racism on those who have suffered physical and verbal abuse and any research on this.

When my children's picture book *My Skin, Your Skin* (*Let's Talk About Race, Racism and Empowerment*), illustrated by Onyinye Iwu, was published, a small percentage of the comments and feedback I received from educators stated that children are too young to have discussions about race and racism. I know from educators and parents that children as young as three have been on the receiving end of racist comments and physical violence, and research informs us that children as young as three can indeed express racial prejudice. We must therefore have age, stage, and ability-appropriate conversations with children on race and racism.

Equally, a few educators have told me that they don't see colour and every child is treated the same. I can see why they make this point and know that it comes from a place of safety and an unwillingness to have a conversation about race as we are 'kind' in Early Years, and everyone is 'lovely'. However, this stance prevents us from talking about what matters and how we can make a difference. When delivering sessions on race and racism, I talk about how not seeing race can be problematic; educators sometimes comment that they never knew it was an issue.

In *Let's Talk About Race in the Early Years*, Stella and Hannah have made sure that educators will have a sound knowledge of race and racism. For some, this will be an introduction to race and racism within the Early Years, and for others it will be another step in their journey in being an anti-racist educator.

This book is particularly important for White educators, especially those White educators who work with Black and Brown children. It is just as important that children who are racialised as White and are looked after by White educators can recognise race and racism and know that they are part of a global village.

I am optimistic and hope that those educators who carefully read and reflect on this book with an open heart and mind will note the personal and professional changes they need to make in their practice and how they will share this with peers, parents, and other key stakeholders, so that the next generation of children becomes anti-racist adults.

I hope you enjoy reading *Let's Talk About Race in the Early Years* as much as I have.

Thank you, Stella, Hannah, Liz, and Nathan, for writing this phenomenal book.

Laura Henry-Allain MBE
Educationalist, Storyteller, Producer, and Consultant

Preface

Hannah Betteridge

When the publishing team at Taylor & Francis approached us to write this book, we, quite literally, jumped at the chance. For both of us, this book has been a long time coming. Our race – as a Black woman and a mixed-race woman – has profoundly affected how we experience the world, and has, at times, unfortunately skewed the lens through which we've seen ourselves.

Like many families, the tragic murder of George Floyd in 2020 acted as a catalyst for a series of very painful discussions about race. As we shared our experiences, we began to notice how the seeds of so many of our experiences began to take root during our childhood. The cumulative experience of a teacher's unconscious and, in some cases, conscious bias; the lack of positive representation; and a curriculum designed to reinforce existing power structures, taught us both who was valued by our society and who was not. (Spoiler alert: we were not.)

My mum (Stella) was born in South London in the late 1960s, raised by hard-working first-generation immigrants who came to the UK from the Commonwealth in search of 'streets paved with gold'. Despite mass advertising, paid for by the UK Government, which actively called for people from the Caribbean to come to the UK to 'rebuild Britain' after the war, the racism they experienced was overt and unrelenting. Thousands of people, including my grandparents, answered the call only to find signs declaring: 'No Blacks. No dogs. No Irish'. As the St Lucian poet Derek Walcott so astutely put it, they quickly came to realise there were 'homecomings without home' (1969). Fast forward 16 years and by the time my mum left school she had been labelled 'unintelligent' and 'trouble'. She was 'loud', 'disruptive', 'aggressive' – a walking embodiment of every negative stereotype thrown her way. Needless to say, these labels were profoundly untrue but true or false, they left lasting self-limiting scars that continue to be felt today.

Nearly 30 years later, I (Hannah) was born in South London in 1993; one month after the tragic murder of Black British teenager Stephen Lawrence, whose life was cut short for no reason other than the colour of his skin. Until this point, my parents hadn't given much thought to how racism might affect me growing up. Times had changed, or so they thought – London was a diverse melting pot of different cultures, racism was no longer tolerated, and representation was on the up, with Diane Abbott becoming the first Black woman elected to the House of Commons in 1987. The death of Stephen Lawrence shattered my parents' reverie, but they still had hope.

Growing up mixed-race (half Black and half White), I have no doubt that my lighter complexion afforded me many privileges, but racism and prejudice still followed me like a dark cloud. In primary school, I was called a 'coconut' and a 'Bounty'. These comments, unchecked by my teachers, stemmed from my love of reading. At the time, I didn't understand what they meant, so I distinctly remember asking my peers why. To this they replied with the utmost confidence: 'Because you're White on the inside and Black on the outside'. The lesson was clear: reading was something you were only supposed to do if you were White. To be truly Black I needed to stop burying my head in books.

Thankfully, my mum fought against this. She encouraged me to continue to devour books, to the point where my suitcase was often filled with more books than clothes when we went on holiday. But I would be lying if I said the seeds of these vitriolic words didn't take root. They instigated a fundamental sense of unease within me, leaving me questioning who I was and where I belonged.

The fact that from primary school to university I only had three Black teachers; I couldn't see people that looked like me in the pages of the books I read; and my naturally curly hair was branded 'unprofessional' in my year nine mock interviews, which were designed to prepare me for the world of work, ultimately provided the nutrients needed for that seed to continue to grow. I am wise enough now to know that, despite what others would have me believe, my academic or professional success was never *in spite* of my Blackness.

Our experiences are not unique. Children are impressionable, and '[o]ne seemingly insignificant experience can shape your life profoundly' (Akala, 2019: 72). As educators, we are placed in a trusted position of power, with a responsibility to act in the best interests of the child. Whether we act consciously or not, our words and our behaviours matter. Without taking the time to examine our own values and biases, we risk putting children in a box of our own making based on what or who we think they should be. We have a moral and ethical duty not only to be aware of the shadow we cast through our words, our actions, or our lack thereof but to challenge discriminatory and prejudicial behaviour when we see it in others. After all, a child should only ever be two things: who and what they want.

Much like my parents in the 1990s, we still like to think times have changed. Whilst some will argue we live in a post-racial society, the harsh reality is that racial inequalities remain entrenched across the Western world. Racism is still alive and kicking, it has just taken a more insidious form. '[It] is like dust in the air. It seems invisible – even if you're choking on it – until you let the sun in', writes NBA legend and community activist Kareem Abdul-Jabbar. 'As long as we keep shining that light, we have a chance of cleaning it wherever it lands' (2020).

Perhaps one of the ultimate ironies is that the word 'race' is pretty straightforward in and of itself – it's just four letters long and takes less than a second to say. However, its meaning and the myriad of experiences that sit underneath its canopy are anything but simple. For some, it stirs up powerful feelings of anger, frustration, or even defensiveness. For others, it can be a source of pride, tiredness, or apathy, or a mixture of all the above at different times in our lives. Regardless of where you sit on this spectrum, one thing is for sure: for something that affects us all, far too many of us are uncomfortable speaking about it.

Our hope is that this book will provide a glimmer of light. Over the next eight chapters, we will give you the tools you need to identify and confront discriminatory or prejudicial practices, whilst growing your confidence in your ability to create dynamic and anti-racist learning environments that embrace and celebrate difference. But we'd be lying if we said this book will provide you with all the answers, nor could it. The lessons you take from this book will ultimately depend on you and the continued effort you put in. It will require action. There may be times when it gets difficult or uncomfortable to read. In those moments, we ask that you sit with that feeling and push through it.

Let's get stuck in.

References

Abdul-Jabbar, K. (2020) 'Op-Ed: Kareem Abdul-Jabbar: Don't Understand the Protests? What You're Seeing is People Pushed to the Edge'. *Los Angeles Times,*

30 May. Available at: https://www.latimes.com/opinion/story/2020-05-30/dont-understand-the-protests-what-youre-seeing-is-people-pushed-to-the-edge.

Akala (2019) *Natives: Race & Class in the Ruins of Empire*. Great Britain: Two Roads.

Walcott, D. (1969) *The Gulf and Other Poems*. London: J. Cape.

Acknowledgements

Writing *Let's Talk About Race in the Early Years* has been a wild ride. Nothing could have prepared us for how emotional the journey to get here would be. To all our friends and family, who shared our tears, anger, and hope, thank you for encouraging us to push ahead, to strive for better and for never letting us feel alone.

Special thanks to Adam Betteridge, for being there every step of the way with endless words of encouragement and support.

To our wonderful contributors, Professor Nathan Holder and Liz Pemberton, thank you for choosing to share this journey with us. It has been a pleasure learning and growing with you.

We are grateful to Stephanie Harding who was always on hand to read through a chapter or two when we needed you most. You were the best critical friend we could have asked for, giving us useful and empowering feedback at every turn. To Julia Manning-Morton, Professor Tina Bruce, Janice Marriot, Kate Razzall and Kathryn Solly, thank you for sharing examples from your practice with us and encouraging us to keep going. To Tia Newell, thank you for being available day and night when it all started to feel like too much.

We would also like to thank the wonderful team at Taylor & Francis, particularly Clare Ashworth and Molly Kavanagh, for their belief in this book and helping us to bring it to life. Thank you for your unrelenting patience when life got in the way and the endless compassion you showed when we needed it most.

1
Introduction
Hannah Betteridge

Before we begin, I have two questions for you. Now, I'll be honest, they're not the easiest questions to answer. In fact, you may even find them a little confronting, but bear with me. The path to being an anti-racist educator is a life-long journey - one that requires bravery, honesty, and a willingness to do better. It will feel tough at times, but one thing is for sure: you will get back what you put in. I promise.

1. When was the last time you had a real and honest conversation about race – one where you actively listened to someone else's point of view, asked, or answered the hard questions, and reflected on or changed your own behaviour as a result?
2. If you were asked to rate how comfortable you feel having conversations about race on a scale of one to ten (with one being that heart racing, blood pumping, get me out of here kind of feeling and ten representing peak relaxation) what would you say?

For most of us, the answers to these questions are probably much longer ago and lower than we would like to admit. If you find yourself in that camp, don't worry. You are not alone. Over the past five years, we have asked these questions in various formats and, in session after session, the highest score people tend to give in response to the second question is six, with many more putting themselves on the lower end of the scale.

I have only ever had one participant triumphantly declare themselves at the top end of the scale with a ten out of ten. When I asked how they got that point and what had contributed to their comfort in these situations, they stated unequivocally that they don't see colour and, as a result, there was no trigger or issue for them to overcome in conversations with others. To

DOI: 10.4324/9781003251149-1

them, race was simply not an issue because they saw and treated everyone the same.

Whilst well intentioned, the so-called 'colour blind' approach that the individual in question had adopted sounded great on paper but was not without its limitations. For a long time, people were encouraged not to see race, as though noticing someone's skin colour made you racist in and of itself. But, if we're truly honest with ourselves, *we all see race*. As young children we're taught the difference between red, purple, and green; we proudly learn and recite all the colours of the rainbow, and adults stop to ask us questions such as 'what colour is that car, train, or bus?' in a bid to further support our learning and development. Why then do we pretend we can't see colour when it comes to race and insist that children do the same?

The truth is that in denying that you see race, you refuse to see me. Now, I want to be clear: my race does not define who I am, nor should it define who I can become, but it is an intrinsic part of me. It shapes both how I move through the world and how parts of the world treat me. Noticing my skin colour does not make you racist, it is the assertion or belief that the colour of my skin makes me more likely to be 'good' or 'bad', 'worthy' or 'not worthy', a 'criminal' or 'innocent', that is racist. Seeing my race and understanding how others may see me as a result does, however, better enable you to engage in the hard conversations about how we achieve anti-racism and understand the role you can play to help us get there as a society.

In adopting a colour-blind approach, people create an illusion of equality which posits that the best way to end racism is to just treat everyone the same. In doing so, the impact and influence of structural and institutional racism are ignored, the prevalence of unconscious biases which we all hold are disregarded, and the individual struggles of people of colour are side-lined. It does not help us move forward and often makes conversations more challenging for people of colour who may feel as though their lived experience is being denied. After all, if you are blind to the problem, how can you hope to find the right solution? Author and educator Jeffrey Boakye, described it perfectly when he said:

> *I don't see colour* is about your comfort, not mine. It's a convenience, to breeze through the corridors and not have to worry about the gravity of racism that pins us all down [...] A community of individuals is a dangerous place to foster blindness. There are too many barbs,

spikes, pitfalls and bear traps lying in wait, laid by a society at large and a history that predates us, to walk around oblivious to the perils. And this is the thing – certain dominant groups have been granted wings with which they can hover over these dangers. Those racialised as white have the privilege of not seeing their own race, because their race has been normalised as 'normal'. Default. Unchallenged and unmaligned…

A school that doesn't see colour is a school that is ideologically unsafe for anyone who is racialised as not-white. It's an environment in which empathy is dull, and in which the seeds of anti-racism cannot hope to embed. There are schools out there that do see colour. I have friends, black, in education who have gone to a new job as the only black member of staff and been taken aside by the headteacher to have a conversation about what to do when racism occurs. *When.* Not 'if'. That's seeing colour. That's allyship.

(Boakye, 2022: 322–323)

This brings me to my third and potentially most significant question of all: why?

- If it has been a long time since your last conversation about race, why is that?
- If you had a conversation more recently, what led to that?
- Irrespective of where you placed yourself on the scale of one to ten, why did you choose the number you did?

Often, we hear that fear of saying or doing the wrong thing is the leading cause of inaction and discomfort when it comes to talking about race. Throughout this book, our goal is to bust myths and eliminate this fear by equipping you with the language and tools to confidently tackle any situation and proactively embed an anti-racist approach into your practice; one that empowers children to understand and celebrate difference and form a positive sense of self. It has been written for *everyone* working in the early years, regardless of your race, background, experience. No prior knowledge is needed. All we ask is that you do the work and we'll be right alongside you, every step of the way.

Why does race matter?

The existence and prevalence of racism are not a universally accepted facts, with some arguing that we live in a post-racial world where all the ills of racism have been overcome and race no longer matters. From my own personal experience, I believe this to be categorically untrue, but the debate about whether race even matters anymore rages on regardless.

Depending on where you are based in the world, you are likely to have different views on the extent to which race and racism remain an issue. For example, a poll conducted by Monmouth University in 2020, showed that 67% of the American public felt that racial and ethnic discrimination in the US is a big problem, while just 17% said it was not a problem at all (Monmouth University, 2020). This is perhaps unsurprising given America's well-known history of slavery and the prominence of Jim Crow laws that enforced segregation across a range of public facilities including schools, buses, restrooms, water fountains, etc., from the late nineteenth century all the way up to 1965 – which, to put into perspective, was less than 60 years ago. Under the presidency of Donald Trump (2017–2021), many commented on the way in which overt racism had once again been legitimised throughout his presidential campaign and time in power, with speeches that riled up hatred towards Mexican immigrants who were demonised as 'rapists' and 'criminals', despite studies showing 'no evidence that immigrants commit more crimes than native-born Americans' (Ye Hee Lee, 2015). And let's not forget his description of members of the Ku Klux Klan (a white supremacist, far-right terrorist organisation with a long history of violence) as 'very fine people' (as quoted in Olusoga, 2020).

However, in the UK, racism is frequently dismissed as a predominantly American problem. I've lost track of the number of people who, throughout the Black Lives Matter movement of 2020, said what happened to George Floyd was terrible but would never happen here. Yet, the killing of Jean Charles de Menezes, a Brazilian man, in 2005 and Chris Kaba, a young Black man, in 2022 are two very real and very notable examples of racial profiling which cost innocent people their lives for no reason other than the colour of their skin. They are not alone; Mark Duggan, Sheku Bayoh, Sean Rigg, Cherry Groce, Leon Briggs, and Christopher Alder all lost their lives at the hands of the UK police and in every single one of these cases their race is believed to have played a contributory factor.

Despite this, the belief we do not have a race problem in the UK persists. Indeed, white actor and politician Lawrence Fox was not alone in holding the view that the UK is 'the most tolerant, lovely country in Europe' (as quoted in Doward, 2020). Even our former Prime Minister, Boris Johnson, who despairingly compared Muslim women wearing a burka to letterboxes and bank robbers, 'does not believe that the UK is a racist country' according to a statement issued by his official spokesperson (Woodcock, 2020). After his own racist remarks, Islamophobic incidents rose by 375% in 2018, with 42% of all Islamophobic incidents which took place on the streets of the UK 'directly referenc[ing] Boris Johnson and/or the language used in his column' (Tell MAMA, 2018: 6).

In many ways, Fox's use of the word 'tolerant' – which means a willingness to *allow, endure, or accept* something that you *dislike* or *disagree* with - tells you all you need to know about British racism. The promotion of diversity and inclusion of people from different races, ethnicities, cultures, and backgrounds is something to be *endured,* not celebrated, accepted, or appreciated. And in *allowing* the presence of people of colour, we continue to preserve a power dynamic predicated on White permission and acceptance for people of colour to exist and take up space.

Britain's history with race and racism is no less complex than America's. It's just less spoken about. Even today, we talk about the British empire as a source of pride, with little understanding of the impact of colonialism including the manmade famines, slave trading, and violent brutality conducted in the name of the state. Despite petitions and protests, neither colonialism nor Black British history is a compulsory part of the curriculum for British primary or secondary school students. When it is taught in schools, the focus is often on Britain's strength and power, and how we spread British values and civilisation to foreign lands, with a de facto assumption that British values were best. We don't talk about the cultures of the countries we took over by force, the state of the countries when we left, or how doing so benefitted our economic interests. For a long time, countries and people were simply viewed as possessions to be had.

We collectively ignore the contributing role that Winston Churchill played in the devastating 1943 Bengal famine, which is estimated to have cost three million people their lives unnecessarily, or his deeply racist belief that Black people were not as 'capable or efficient' or efficient as White people (Toye, 2011: 2), simply because of his wartime victory over Adolf Hitler.[1]

Our unwillingness to critically examine Churchill (and many others like him) means that we are incapable as a nation of acknowledging the complexity of human behaviour – someone can be both good and bad; they can effectively champion the interests of their own whilst not protecting or prioritising the interests of others. Yes, Winston Churchill demonstrated incredible resilience and leadership as a prime minister, but he also held deeply damaging and racist views that affected the choices he made. Until we accept that, we cannot fully understand and appreciate the power dynamics and structures at play that have historically protected and perpetuated vast disparities in the treatment of people of colour.

Isn't racism a thing of the past?

Today, the legacy of our colonial past can still be felt in every echelon of society, with study and study highlighting that the colour of your skin continues to have a far-reaching impact on your experiences and outcomes in the UK. If we take a look at the data trends across four key pillars of daily life - housing, education, employment, and health – it is abundantly clear that racism continues to be a significant and enduring problem of our time.

- **Housing** – access to safe and secure housing is often viewed as an important determinant of your health, wellbeing, and quality of life. Whilst the days of landlords posting signs saying 'No Irish, no blacks, no dogs' are thankfully long gone, research conducted by Generation Rent in 2023 showed that racism and discrimination continue to be embedded within the housing sector.

  To test whether race played a factor in access to decent housing, Generation Rent conducted an experiment by setting up two profiles of would-be tenants on Spare Room (a platform designed to find flat or house shares). The profiles were identical in all but name and ethnicity – one profile picture depicted a Black woman and the other a White woman. They found that the White profile was 36% more likely to receive a positive response and 17% more likely to receive any response at all when compared to the Black profile, despite sending identical messages. Interestingly, Generation Rent noted that: 'More common however were subtler uses of gatekeeping to view properties, with screening questions sent to the Black facing profile and immediate positive responses to viewing requests sent to the white facing profile' (2023). These findings are not new or shocking and highlight the prevalence of a more subtle form of prejudice that is still common in the UK. It also echoes many studies that come before it, including Shelter's 2021 survey which found that Black and Asian people are disproportionately likely to face discrimination whilst looking for a home (Shelter, 2021).

- **Employment** – for many of us, a secure well-paid job is the only thing keeping us above the poverty line. Whilst there may be things about our jobs that we dislike, we expect to be able to work into walk every day, be treated with respect, and judged only by the content of our performance, not the colour of our skin. However, in 2022, the Trade Union Congress conducted vital research into the treatment of Black and ethnic minority employees in the UK. Their vital report, *Still Rigged: Racism in the UK Labour Market*, showed that more than two in five Black, Brown and minority ethnic employees in the UK say they have faced racism in the workplace in the last five years, including overhearing racist jokes, being subject to racist remarks, comments on their appearance, or being subject to bullying and harassment (Trade Union Congress, 2022: 7). Based on the quantitative data they analysed, they ultimately concluded that 'racism scars every aspect of working life. As well as determining who gets hired and fired, it also shapes Black workers day-to-day experiences, from training and promotion opportunities to the allocation of shifts and holidays' (Trade Union Congress, 2022: 3).

In my own personal experience, racism in the workplace is often insidious and hard to describe. I have frequently experienced White colleagues assume just from looking at me that I am an administrative assistant, only present in a meeting to take notes. They glide past me ignoring my existence and walk over to the junior White members of my team, asking if there are ready to begin. Thankfully, my team have almost always instinctively corrected this behaviour, pointing to me, and introducing me as their head of team. This usually elicits a slightly awkward and embarrassed response of: 'I'm sorry, I didn't see you there'. I have held roles where I have always been confused with the one other person of colour in the wider team, who looks nothing like me and whose name sounds nothing like mine, despite having worked with and led meetings with these people for years. I have turned to senior colleagues for help when a racist incident has occurred only to be told that they don't think it's necessary to send out communications highlighting we take a zero-tolerance approach to racism. There is a constant fear that if you push the matter too hard or make too much of a fuss your card will be marked, and you'll been seen as just another angry Black woman. These incidents gradually chip away at you day after day, undermining your confidence and sense of self-worth. And yet, as a mixed-race woman I am consciously aware that my lighter skin has afforded me a degree of privilege; the experiences of my Black friends and family have often been far worse. Navigating the workplace as a person of colour is tiring; the expectation remains that you need to work twice as hard for half as much.

- **Education** – as we will discuss throughout this book, the education system in the UK continues to be a breeding ground for racism, which affects outcomes and prevents every child from being able to reach their full potential. The workforce is overwhelmingly White, with 46% of schools found to have no teachers from minority ethnic groups by University College London in 2020 (Tereshchenko *et al.*, 2020: 8). This has an impact of the visibility of role models and impacts racial literacy in schools. Teachers from minority ethnic backgrounds are also underrepresented in leadership roles, with just seven per cent of primary school headteachers from an ethnic minority background in 2020 (Department for Education, 2022: 16). This striking lack of representation risks children of colour internalising an unspoken message that they are less suited to leadership positions and is only further compounded by the absence of Black British history from the curriculum, which provides yet another signal to children of colour that they are less important than their White counterparts.

In addition, the culture we cultivate in schools can be damaging to a young child's developing sense of self, leaving children of colour feeling inadequate by centring and emphasising Whiteness as the norm. A report conducted by the YMCA in 2020 found that young Black people felt the need to change themselves to be "accepted" by society, with 70% saying they needed to change the texture of their hair be "more professional" at work or at school (YMCA, 2020: 7). In focus groups, 'they shared experiences of teachers suggesting that Black Afro-textured hair is "untidy" and "needed to be brushed", while young black men spoke of hair policies at school being "just another form of racism" by not being inclusive of young Black people' (YMCA, 2020: 14). Examples were given of teachers penalising those that didn't comply with these appearance policies, and, at times, they would publicly make an example of them in front of their peers. The study also found that 50% of those polled felt teacher perceptions were one of the biggest barriers to young Black people achieving at school (YMCA, 2020: 14). As we will go on to discuss in detail in Chapter 2, the unconscious bias held by teachers has been proven to have a profoundly negative impact on educational attainment, assessment outcomes, and disciplinary measures for decades, with Black children placed at a significant disadvantage (Coard, 2021).

• **Health** – significant racial disparities also exist across our healthcare system. For example, we know that Black women are four times more likely to die in pregnancy and childbirth than White women. Stillbirth rates for babies of Black ethnicity are over twice as high as those for babies of White ethnicity, and Black women are 40% more likely to experience a miscarriage than their White counterparts (Tommy's, 2022). Despite such disparities being documented for over 20 years, it is interesting to note that they only began to attract mainstream attention and Government action around 2018 (Women and Equalities Committee, 2023: 3). This raises important questions about whose lives we deem to be valuable and more deserving of investment and intervention.

However, such disparities are not confined to maternal medicine. There is a wide range of evidence which draws attention to the fact that a substantial number of medical professionals hold false beliefs or about biological differences between Black and White patients, dating back to slavery (e.g., that Black people have thicker skin than White people), particularly where it comes to pain perception. This has been shown to affect not only the way in which Black people are treated but also the accuracy of treatment recommendations (Hoffman et al., 2016). Black and brown skin is also rarely represented in medical training and textbooks, which tend to focus almost exclusively on White people, often leading to missed or false diagnosis and inequalities in care and treatment for people of colour (Hurynag, 2020).

During the coronavirus pandemic, racial disparities once again came to the fore with data showing that Black people were almost twice as likely to die from Covid-19 than White people, even once other variables such as ages, measures of self-reported health and disability, and sociodemographic characteristics were taken into account (Office for National Statistics, 2020). The factors behind this are still yet to be properly understood. However, the lack of diversity amongst those making decisions – both in Government and key advisory groups such as the Scientific Advisory Group for Emergencies (SAGE) who were responsible for advising ministers during the pandemic, is believed to have played a role. Key lifesaving equipment was designed with Whiteness in mind, with researchers at the University of Southampton concluding that most face masks were not designed to fit Black and ethnic minority women, putting them at significant risk (Chopra *et al.*, 2021).

Similar trends can be seen in housing, employment, education, and health data across the Western world. We need to stop pretending that racism is only a problem in countries far, far away; that it's someone else's problem. Racism is and remains a global issue. You can see it in the dehumanising and inflammatory language used to describe 'immigrants' who almost always have Black or Brown skin compared to White 'expats', in the popularisation of the 'war on woke', as though it's better to be asleep to issues than awake, and in the resurgence of far-right political groups from the Netherlands to Australia.

As you read these studies, it can be easy to forget that behind each of these statistics is a person whose life has been impacted, and the cumulative impact should not be underestimated; these experiences stack on top of each other, one after another, like death by a thousand paper cuts. As children of colour grow up and move through the world, they will witness their mothers, fathers, brothers, and sisters be impacted by these issues, and the chances are they will also be directly affected themselves. They will absorb the implicit messages underlying each interaction, which centres Whiteness as the default and, without support, we know that this can lead to low self-esteem and cause significant trauma that further impacts on their health and wellbeing.

But aren't they too young?

The idea that children don't see race is something we come across a lot in training sessions and interactions with practitioners and parents. Often, this belief prevents adults from discussing race with children and is coupled with quite strongly held beliefs that children are too innocent to discuss something as horrible as racism. However, studies have shown that by the time babies turn three months old they start to demonstrate a 'significant preference' for faces from their own ethnic group and therefore the race they're most likely exposed to, highlighting that a child's initial awareness of racial difference starts from a very young age (Kelly *et al.*, 2005). Between the ages of six to nine months old, we can see bias beginning to form, with babies associating faces from their race with happy music and faces of those from other races with sad music due, in part, to a lack of exposure to people of other races (Xiao *et al.*, 2017). By the age of two to three, children use racial categories to reason about others and interpret and explain their behaviour (Hirschfeld, 2008: 39). At this point, we tend to see children interpret behaviours in line with the stereotypes held by adults, with 'Three-year-olds generally attribut[ing] positive properties to members of the majority race, whereas 5-year-olds not only attribute positive properties to [the] majority race, but also negative properties to minority races' (Hirschfeld, 2008: 39; see also Clark and Clark, 1947).

Racial prejudice is not just something that 'bad' people hold; it is something that is effortlessly and unconsciously learned at a young age, without malice or deliberate intent. When we present Whiteness as the norm and everything else as other in every single structure of our society, it is unsurprising that children pick up on these cues and internalise them. They are, after all, products of their environment. Educators need to be cognisant of how quickly stereotypes can take root and biases can form if we are going to effectively prepare children to navigate the world around them. If we don't, we are setting children up to fail. Ignoring racism does not stop it from existing; it just stops children from being able to call it out and deal with it. As Dr Pragya Agarwal argues:

> When we do not talk about race and identity actively, children are more likely to internalise any racism, and form a negative view of themselves; they are more likely to pick up stereotypes about people and incorrectly judge them; and they can be unsure of how to tackle any racially charged words and actions targeted at them or others around them.
>
> (Agarwal, 2020: 9)

That is why it is so important that we give children a positive frame of reference to counter the negative views and experiences that lie in wait and prepare children to be allies that actively champion, celebrate, and respect difference.

The power of language

Before we can hope to support children to understand race, it is important that we understand the ways that race and racism work in society and have the language to discuss the issues at play without causing offence. Described below are some of the most common words or phrases you are likely to come across to help prepare you on your journey and make you feel more equipped to dive in.

Allyship

A few years ago, I was in the middle of a training session when someone turned to a White colleague of mine who was co-delivering the session with me and asked what being an ally meant to him. In response, he said something that has stuck with me ever since: 'Allyship is a verb, not a noun. Being an ally is not an identity; it is something that necessitates action. It's about both *what* I do and *how* I do it'.

To be an ally, you have to commit to understanding and recognising any privilege you may have on the basis of your gender, class, race, sexual orientation, etc., and work in genuine partnership with marginalised groups to actively challenge problematic behaviour, whether at an individual or societal level. When it comes to race, it is not just about opening up conversations, it's about how you centre and amplify the voices and experiences of people of colour in those conversations. Likewise, it's not just about committing to learning about race and racism, it's about taking personal responsibility and accountability for doing so. Learning about race does not mean asking your Black and Brown colleagues and/or friends to send you resources or answer all your questions. It is not the job of already marginalised and oppressed groups to educate you; placing that expectation on them simply increases the burden they are expected to carry.

There are, however, different types of allyship. Throughout the Black Lives Matter movement of 2020, I witnessed a lot of performative allyship. People were quick to post a black square on social media to symbolise their solidarity with the cause but were rarely as quick to check their privilege and make real change. True allyship is a proactive, continuous, and extraordinarily challenging process of learning and unlearning; it is not about who sees you take action (Mosby Tyler, 2020). My challenge to you is to ask yourself: what do you do when nobody is watching, when the news cycle changes and the pressure to stand up and be counted is gone?

BAME/BME

'BAME' and 'BME' are two commonly used acronyms which stand for Black, Asian and Minority Ethnic and Black and Minority Ethnic respectively. Researchers, governments, and organisations have used these acronyms as a catch-all term when referring to ethnic minority groups for a long time. However, in the last few years, there has been a growing recognition that the use of these acronyms can be more harmful than helpful. After all, Black, Asian and Minority Ethnic communities are not a homogeneous group – the experience of someone who identifies as Black Caribbean will be vastly different from someone who identifies as Bengali or Black African for that matter.

In grouping such a large proportion of people together by default, we hide a myriad of experiences and inhibit our ability to find meaningful solutions to real-world issues. If you take data on the rates of permanent exclusion from schools as an example, you'll get one statistic if you look at the total number of 'BAME' students who have been excluded, but you'll get a very different set of statistics if you look at the number of students who have been excluded from school by individual ethnicity. Typically, the data tends to show disproportionately high rates of exclusions amongst Black Caribbean children, with the lowest rates of exclusions found amongst Chinese and Indian pupils – two polar opposite trends under the same umbrella of 'BAME' (Department for Education, 2023). As an educator or policymaker, if I choose to only look at what the data shows for 'BAME' children as a collective, I can't see what is really going on. My perception of the issue and therefore the solution I pursue will vary significantly according to the granularity of the data I am looking at.

Often, people use 'BAME' and 'BME' colloquially to describe anyone who isn't White, and yet 'ethnic minority' is defined by the Oxford English Dictionary as 'a group within a country or community which has different national or cultural traditions from the larger, dominant population' (2023). In most Western societies, this definition would therefore include the Jewish community and Gypsy, Roma, and Traveller community – a fact which is often not understood (Louis, 2020).

Throughout this book, we only use the terms 'BAME' and 'BME' where quoting directly from other sources that have used this language, including statistical research, where disaggregated data is not available due to the data collection methods used at the time. However, if you are having a conversation about race in your setting, we would encourage you to recognise the limitations of this approach and be specific and deliberate in your choice of language. If there's an issue affecting Chinese children in your setting, say that. If there's an issue affecting Pakistani children in your setting, say that. Hiding behind umbrella terms muddies the issue and leads to us adopting generic solutions, but generic solutions to specific problems rarely work.

Black Lives Matter

Suggesting that 'Black lives matter' does not negate the value of other lives, nor does it suggest that Black lives matter more than any others. However, as one law professor put it, the issue is that people often perceive there to be 'an invisible "only" in front of the words 'Black Lives Matter'' when no such qualifier exists. He goes on to explain that, 'There is a difference between *focus* and *exclusion* [emphasis added]. If something matters, this does not imply that nothing else does' (as quoted in Lopez, 2016).

In a world where Black lives are routinely and deliberately targeted and undervalued, Black Lives Matter is an ideological and political intervention designed to focus minds and target attention to a particular group whose lives have been undervalued by the systems and structures surrounding us for far too long, including, as in the case of George Floyd, by those that are designed to keep us safe. For years, studies have shown that Black people are treated with deadly force far more often than White people and, in those situations, authorities are held less accountable (Bunn, 2022). We also know that in equivalent situations, Black people receive prison sentences that are nearly 20% longer than White people for the same crimes (United States

Sentencing Commission, 2017). Yet, I think we can all agree that your risk of being brutalised by the police or receiving a longer prison sentence should not be greater simply because you happen to be born Black, not White.

Of course, all lives matter. Nobody is saying that they don't. All they are saying is that Black lives matter, too. To help explain why responding to 'Black Lives Matter' with statements like 'No, all lives matter' is so unhelpful and unnecessary, a few cartoons and memes went viral in 2020 which substituted lives for houses to take the emotion out of it. The premise behind these images was essentially to encourage people to ask themselves what they would do if their neighbour's house was on fire and the fire brigade were called out to put out the fire. In that situation, would you and your neighbours march out to the firefighters and ask: 'What about our houses? Why haven't you poured a little water over ours, too? All houses on the street matter!'? I highly doubt it. If your house isn't on fire and there is no immediate danger that means your house needs specific and targeted attention to address a direct and imminent risk, the chances are you would be fine letting your neighbour's house receive the attention it needed to put out the flames and make sure everyone was safe.

Cultural appropriation

In her seminal TED Talk, *Cultural Appropriation: Why Your Pocahontas Costume Isn't Okay*, Aaliyah Jihad defines cultural appropriation as 'the act of adopting symbols, practices, etc., of historically oppressed target groups of people by members of the privileged agent group' (Jihad, 2014). There are two necessary components: first, an unequal power dynamic between a powerful or dominant group who 'borrows' from a minority group without any of the negative ramifications or perceptions that are often levied at the minority group for doing or wearing the same thing, and second, a lack of understanding or appreciation of the cultural context and significance of the object being appropriated, which often only serves to perpetuate harmful stereotypes (Vollans, 2017).

The line between what is and isn't cultural appropriation can be confusing, with critics dismissing the concept as political correctness gone mad. But just because something is complex does not mean we shouldn't engage in the conversation, particularly when someone is telling us that action has caused offence. Ignoring these voices is just another way in which we consciously or unconsciously sideline the experience of minority groups in society to protect the comfort of White dominant groups. To bring the issue to light, Ohio University ran several powerful poster campaigns in 2012 and 2013 which shine a light on the impact of cultural appropriation on the groups of people whose culture is being appropriated. The posters read, 'We're a culture, not a costume' and 'You wear a costume for one night. I wear the stigma for life'.

In early years settings, the risk of cultural appropriation is generally the greatest in the dressing up corner or around holidays, such as Halloween. If you were to look at the role play box in your setting, what items of clothing would you find in there?

- Does anything in there mock a certain culture or group or reinforce stereotypes?
- Does using any of the items in there trivialise or reduce someone's culture?
- Do any of the items in there hold cultural significance?
- How might removing an item from the context from which it was origi-nally intended and placing it in a different setting (e.g., a dressing up box in this case) change its meaning?

Encouraging children to 'try on' and play 'dress up' with different cultures without context or meaning does not breed mutual respect and understanding between children of different cultures; instead, it simply devalues aspects of someone's culture. Two common examples of cultural appropriation include the use of Native American war bonnets (sometimes called headdresses by other cultures) or Rastafarian hats with fake dreadlocks attached. In both cases, these items carry a significant amount of symbolic importance to the cultures they originate from. Dreadlocks, for example, are spiritually significant to Rastafarians for whom they symbolise a connection to God, whilst Native American war bonnets are a symbol of bravery and honour and are reserved for those who have earned great respect in their tribe. Neither are fashion accessories to be worn in a bid to be seen as edgy or exotic, or for a bit of fun. Introducing children to different cultures should be done in a meaningful and thoughtful way – one which cultivates mutual respect and understanding. As Vollans argues, 'When children have seen how things are used in real-life situations, their play will be much richer – and so will their learning' (2017).

Diversity vs inclusion

Verna Myers, a leading diversity and inclusion specialist, once said, 'Diversity is being invited to the party. Inclusion is being asked to dance' (as quoted in Cho, 2016). In this context, diversity simply means a range of different things or people coming together. It covers both similarities and differences in the following areas: nationality, educational and/or socioeconomic background, language, gender, sexual orientation, age, ethnicity, disability, and so forth. Inclusion is about how we create environments where people feel like they belong, where they can be their true, authentic self without needing to wear a mask or code switch to be accepted, valued, or respected. For this reason, diversity is meaningless without inclusion. What is the point in being invited to the table if my voice is not going to be heard? To me, true inclusion goes beyond Myers' description – being *asked* to dance still places the power in the hands of the person asking me. Instead, inclusion is being involved in the planning, having a say in the music, the food, etc.; it is knowing your views will be listened to and heard (Juday, 2017).

In recent years, there has been a growing acknowledgement and acceptance of the need for diversity and inclusion in the workplace. Bringing in different perspectives is not just good for society but also makes economic sense, with companies with more diverse workforces found to perform better financially. Indeed, in their 2015 report, *Diversity Matters*, Hunt, Layton, and Prince showed that the companies that ranked in the top 25% for gender diversity were 15% more likely to have financial returns above their national industry median. For those in the top 25% for racial and ethnic diversity, the numbers shot up to 35% more likely to have greater financial returns than their national industry median (Hunt *et al.*, 2015: 1).

Children that grow up without exposure to diversity will grow up with a very limited narrow world view, making them ill-equipped in today's society. Inclusion and diversity should be embedded into the fabric of our settings to build up children's understanding of and respect for different cultures; it needs to be built into our workforce, policies, resources, and lesson plans. Without this, we make it hard for children to develop the ability to interact and relate to people that are different from themselves. We make it more likely that stereotypes will take hold and therefore create a breeding ground for intolerance, prejudice, and discrimination.

Equality vs equity

Equality is about treating everyone equally, irrespective of their gender, race, ethnicity, religion, socioeconomic background, sexuality, or any other individual difference. It means giving every person the same opportunities, rights, and status. By contrast, equity starts by recognising that life is not a level playing field – for example, it acknowledges that some children are born into poverty, whilst others are born into wealth which brings with it a series of advantages. If life were a race, both children would not be starting from the same position – the child born into wealth would have a significant head start and face fewer hurdles in getting to the finish line. To address this, an approach based on equity would allocate resources to each child based on need to support both children in reaching an equal outcome. Equity argues that treating everyone equally ignores the structural inequalities present within our society, including socioeconomic and racial disadvantage.

Ethnicity

Ethnicity refers to a person's identity based on their cultural experiences, religion, language, nationality, ancestral history, and way of life. For example, I would describe my ethnicity as mixed – Black Caribbean and White British, whilst a White person might describe their ethnicity as Irish, Italian, French, Spanish, etc.

However, often, people use the terms race and ethnicity interchangeably. As Agarwal explains:

> It is very tricky to disentangle race and ethnicity, and people may find themselves being given a racial identity in society that overrides their ethnicity. For instance, a person coming from the Indian subcontinent might identify as being Indian, Tamil, Bengali, Bangladeshi, Pakistani or Nepali, based on language or national identities, but they are very likely to be all seen as 'brown' or 'Asian' in the UK or US first and foremost.
>
> (2020: 27)

Microaggression

Microaggressions (sometimes referred to as microincivilities or microassaults) are brief and commonplace verbal or behavioural indignities that are indirect and subtle prejudicial slights, often underpinned by negative attitudes towards marginalised groups (Sue *et al.*, 2007: 271). They can be intentional or unintentional. Examples include:

- 'Where are you from?' – I have lost count of the number of times I have been asked this question, including by strangers who have felt that it is appropriate to come up to me in the middle of the street and ask. My reply is always the same, 'England'. This often elicits a perplexed facial expression and a further probe of, 'No, where are you *really* from?'. To which I restate my previous answer, 'England. Both of my parents were born here'. Sometimes people stop here, as they begin to realise the absurdity of their question, but others keep pressing. It's a loaded question and one that carries with it an explicit implication that this (in my case, England) is not and cannot be my home. It is a way of othering someone.
- 'You are so articulate' or 'you speak well' – These statements, although generally intended as complements, carry with them an implicit undertone that it is unusual for someone of your race or ethnicity to be well spoken. In my experience this is sometimes followed by statements, such as 'You don't sound Black'.
- Touching or asking to touch a Black person's hair – This invasive microaggression perpetuates the idea White European hair is the norm and everything else is other – something exotic to be experienced. Black people are not there to be petted for the sake of someone's curiosity.
- Clutching your handbag or crossing over to the other side of the street when you see a Black person – This action carries with it a presumption that Black people are dangerous, criminals, or people to be fearful of. It therefore perpetuates harmful stereotypes and is hugely offensive.

These are just some examples – the list of commonplace microaggressions is far more extensive and wide-ranging than we have space to cover in this book. For people of colour, these comments and/or incidents often happen throughout their life, starting from a very young age. They can affect your wellbeing, self-worth, and sense of belonging.

Prejudice

Prejudice can be defined as the preconceived ideas and beliefs we hold, consciously or unconsciously, about particular groups of people. They are usually heavily influenced by stereotypes, as well as by what we observe and hear from others. For example, someone may have preconceived notions about someone who is Black, White, or Asian and treat people differently as a result. Racism is a form of prejudice, as is sexism, ageism, classism, homophobia, Islamophobia, anti-Semitism, and xenophobia.

Race

You may have heard people say race is a social construct, not a biological reality, but what does this really mean? Well, scientists have proven that human beings share approximately 99.9% of our genetic code with one another, and whilst genetic tests can be conducted to find out more about your ancestry (e.g., where our ancestors geographically originated from), there is no way of determining or verifying someone's race. Race does not exist in human biology.

However, race still plays an important role in our society. It is a powerful way of categorising people based on physical characteristics, primarily on the basis of skin colour, which has historically been used to control and oppress different groups. The racial category that you are assigned to can confer either advantage or disadvantage, inclusion or exclusion, and power or oppression.

Racism

Racism occurs when someone experiences discrimination or prejudice on the basis of their race, skin tone, nationality, ethnicity, or ancestry. At an individual level, racism can be seen through someone's general attitude and dislike of a certain race or group of people with particular characteristics, and these beliefs may influence their behaviours and actions. It can be overt, like the use of racial slurs or threats directed at particular groups, or covert, present in subtle microaggressions that promote stereotypes or inappropriate Halloween costumes. As educators, it is important that we constructively oppose and question racism wherever and whenever we see it. Your setting should have policies and procedures in place to support you through this.

Institutional racism (sometimes referred to as systemic racism) is used to describe all of the deeply ingrained policies and practices entrenched in established institutions that harm certain racial groups and help others. In education, you can see institutional racism at play in the Eurocentric curriculum and the setting of appearance policies that shame and exclude Black hair. It can also be present in the application and admission process, as Jane Lane explains:

> 'An early years setting that operates a waiting list and offers places on a first-come-first-served basis, with those at the top of the list having priority, may well be operating institutional racism. At first sight the waiting list seems as fair a method as any, but [...] people who are unfamiliar with the system are likely to include families:

- For whom English is not the first language
- That have recently arrived in Britain or do not yet know about early years organisations – are not part of the 'system'
- [...] The waiting list will disproportionately affect Travellers, Roma and Gypsies; refugees, asylum seekers and other migrants; South Asian and some other minority ethnic families; as well as majority or minority ethnic families moving to the area'. To address this, 'a setting could consider holding back a small number of places to cater for transient families or late arrivals, especially where it is known that some communities may settle temporarily but regularly'.

(2008: 35–36)

Helpful resource

In her comprehensive book, *Young Children and Racial Justice*, Jane Lane provides a helpful two-page checklist to support settings in monitoring their practice and procedures for institutional racism (see page 38–29).

Structural racism, by contrast, is what happens when all of these institutions come together and overlap; it is the cumulative impact of dozens, or hundreds, or thousands of people [and institutions] with the same biases joining together […] and acting accordingly. Structural racism is an impenetrably white workplace culture, where anyone who falls outside the cultural norm must conform or face failure, or views certain traits as 'professional' or 'unprofessional'.

(Eddo-Lodge, 2018: 64)

If racism is to be eradicated, we need to look not just at individual behaviour, but at the series of institutional and structural advantages and disadvantages that exist for some groups and not others and address them.

White privilege

White privilege has become an incredibly controversial term in recent years, which is used to describe the inherent and relative advantages that White people benefit from simply by virtue of their race. In her ground-breaking essay, *Unpacking the Invisible Knapsack,* Peggy McIntosh describes her own experience of coming to terms with White privilege and her understanding of the concept:

As a white person, I realized I had been taught about racism as something that puts others at a disadvantage, but had been taught not to see one of its corollary aspects, white privilege, which puts me at an advantage […] I have come to see white privilege as an invisible package of unearned assets that I can count on cashing in each day […] like an invisible knapsack of special provisions, maps, passports, codebooks, visas, clothes, tools and blank checks.

(1989)

When you are born into this type of privilege, it can be difficult to see it or understand it, especially when Whiteness is presented so effectively as the norm in our society that it becomes the neutral, default position. After all, if you move through the world never being or made to be consciously aware of your race, it is easy to see how you can be blind to its benefits, but that does not mean the benefits aren't there. White privilege is never having to question what it means to be White, or waste energy worrying about what preconceived assumptions or beliefs other people have about them and how they may be treated as a result. It's turning on the TV or flicking through the pages of a book and seeing people that look like you. It's the fact that White history is taught as part of the core curriculum, whilst Black history is an optional extra. It's not being racially profiled by the police as a criminal or having to talk to your children about what to do if they are stopped and searched to avoid heightening the perception that they are a threat. It's being seen as an individual with your own thoughts, interests, and abilities rather than a homogenous blob. It is a series of structural advantages embedded into the fabric of our society.

Accepting White privilege does not dismiss the cross section of struggle that comes from class disadvantage or any of the other disadvantages or difficulties you may face in your life. It simply seeks to highlight how race is a barrier that being White means you are free from. That does not mean that you will not have your own struggles, but it does mean that you have one thing that you don't need to worry about: your race.

White supremacy

White supremacy can be defined as the idea or belief that White people are superior to people of colour and therefore have an intrinsic right to lead and govern society, typically to the exclusion or detriment of anyone who is not White. It has historically been accompanied by a belief that White people should live by themselves in segregated societies, and that White people are genetically superior to other people.

However, sociologists argue that White supremacy is more than this. It is not just predicated on the assumption that White people are superior and therefore confined to extremist far-right groups like the Ku Klux Klan. White supremacy promotes White people 'as the norm or standard for human, and people of colour as an inherent deviation from that norm' (DiAngelo, 2017). Under this view, White supremacy can be seen in the way we, as a society, automatically ascribe value and morality to Whiteness, with connotations of purity and innocence, whilst depicting people of colour as immoral, worthless, and undeserving. Indeed, throughout our society, darkness is presented as something to be feared.

The rhetoric used to describe human migration, which is mentioned elsewhere in this chapter, perfectly captures the way in which racial hierarchies are still enforced today. In this context, White people, for example, are commonly referred to as 'expats' or 'migrants' – the moral, social, and economic benefit they bring to the recipient country is implicit, expected, and normalised. The term 'immigrants' is instead typically reserved by those in positions of power to describe those deemed to be inferior and often accompanied by divisive language that is designed to pit 'them' against 'us', with statements such as *'they* are coming to steal *our* jobs' or 'scrounge off benefits'.

As educators, it is important that we call out White supremacy where we see it and seek to challenge the assumption that Whiteness is the norm. To do this, we need to understand where it is at play, name it, and tackle it head on. We need to teach children the value of other cultures and encourage difference to be both respected and celebrated in the physicality and content of our settings.

Building your anti-racist practice

All educators have a moral and ethical pedagogical responsibility to support every child in thriving, to help them build a positive self-identity, and to shape their understanding of the world. We cannot do this effectively without a sound awareness and understanding of the role and impact of race and racism in our society. Until we take the time to understand our own prejudice, the dangers of tokenism, and how all these things manifest, we cannot truly assess or support the holistic needs of the child.

Throughout the rest of this book, we will build on the concepts discussed in this chapter and explore how you can create dynamic and inclusive learning environments in the early years that embrace difference, prevent stereotypes from taking root, and equip children with the ideas and knowledge they need to make sense of the world around them. Each chapter will focus on a different element of your practice – from bias in the assessment, observation, and planning process through to the physicality of your settings – with examples and exercises to guide you through the process step by step.

Whilst the road to being an anti-racist educator is long and can be uncomfortable at times, it will be worth it. Now is the time for us to do better, push harder, and go further.

Note

1 Winston Churchill served as Conservative Prime Minister twice – from 1940 to 1945 and again from 1951 to 1955. He is generally revered as one of the greatest Brits of all time and one of the most popular and successful British Prime Ministers.

References

Agarwal, P. (2020) *Wish We Knew What to Say: Talking with Children about Race*. London. Dialogue Books.

Boakye, J. (2022) *I Heard What You Said: A Black Teacher, A White System, A Revolution in Education*. London: Picador.

Bunn, C. (2022) 'Report: Black People Are Still Killed by Police at a Higher Rate than Other Groups'. *NBC News*, 3 March 2022. Available at: https://www.ussc.gov/sites/default/files/pdf/research-and-publications/research-publications/2017/20171114_Demographics.pdf.

Cho, J.H. (2016) '"Diversity Is Being Invited to the Party; Inclusion Is Being Asked to Dance," Verna Myers Tells Cleveland Bar'. *Cleveland*, 25 May 2016. Available at: https://www.cleveland.com/business/2016/05/diversity_is_being_invited_to.html.

Chopra, J., Abiakam, N, Kim, H., Metcalf, C., Worsley, P. and Cheong, Y. (2021) 'The Influence of Gender and Ethnicity on Facemasks and Respiratory Protective Equipment Fit: A Systematic Review and Meta-analysis'. *British Medical Journal Global Health*, 6, p. e005537.

Clark, K.B. and Clark, M.P. (1947) 'Racial Identification and Preference in Negro Children'. In T.M. Newcomb and E.L. Hartley (eds.) *Readings in Social Psychology*. New York: Rinehart & Winston, pp. 602–611.

Coard, B. (2021) *How the West Indian Child Is Made Educationally Sub-Normal in the British School System*. Expanded 5th edn. Kingston: McDermott Publishing.

Department for Education (2022) *School Leadership in England 2010 to 2020: Characteristics and Trends*. Available at: https://assets.publishing.service.gov.uk/media/626950bfe90e0746c0a7b057/School_leadership_in_England_2010_to_2020_characteristics_and_trends_-_report.pdf.

Department for Education (2023) *Permanent Exclusions by Ethnicity: 2020–21 School Year*. Available at: https://www.ethnicity-facts-figures.service.gov.uk/education-skills-and-training/absence-and-exclusions/permanent-exclusions/latest/#permanent-exclusions-by-ethnicity.

DiAngelo, R. (2017) 'No, I Won't Stop Saying "White Supremacy"'. *Yes!* 30 June 2017. Available at: https://www.yesmagazine.org/democracy/2017/06/30/no-i-wont-stop-saying-white-supremacy.

Doward, J. (2020) 'Lecturer Says She Faced Online Abuse after Question Time Clash with Laurence Fox'. *The Guardian*, 18 January 2020. Available at: https://www.

theguardian.com/tv-and-radio/2020/jan/18/question-time-clash-lecturer-tells-of-hate-mail.

Eddo-Lodge, R. (2018) *Why I'm No Longer Talking to White People about Race.* London: Bloomsbury.

Generation Rent (2023) *Minority Ethnic People More Likely to Be Ignored when Searching for New Privately Rented Homes.* Available at: https://www.generationrent.org/2023/11/08/minority-ethnic-people-more-likely-to-be-ignored-when-searching-for-new-privately-rented-homes/.

Hirschfeld, L.A. (2008) 'Children's Developing Conceptions of Race'. In S.M. Quintana and C. McKown (eds.) *Handbook of Race, Racism, and the Developing Child.* Hoboken, NJ: John Wiley & Sons, pp. 37–54.

Hoffman, K.M., Trawalter, S., Axt, J.R. and Oliver, M.N. (2016) 'Racial Bias in Pain Assessment and Treatment Recommendations, and False Beliefs about Biological Differences Between Blacks and Whites'. *Proceedings of the National Academy of Sciences,* 113(16) (19 April), pp. 4296–4301.

Hunt, V., Layton, D. and Prince, S. (2015) *Diversity Matters.* McKinsey & Company. Available at: https://www.mckinsey.com/~/media/mckinsey/business%20functions/people%20and%20organizational%20performance/our%20insights/why%20diversity%20matters/diversity%20matters.pdf.

Hurynag, A. (2020) 'Doctors May Be Missing Illnesses because UK Medical Textbooks Often Focus on White People'. *Sky News,* 10 July 2020. Available at: https://news.sky.com/story/doctors-may-be-missing-illnesses-because-uk-medical-textbooks-often-focus-on-white-people-12025268.

Jihad, A. (2014) 'Cultural Appropriation: Why Your Pocahontas Costume Isn't Okay: Aaliyah Jihad at TEDxYouth@AnnArbor'. *YouTube,* 6 May 2014. Available at: https://www.youtube.com/watch?v=zSV7Hi2eYLQ.

Juday, D. (2017) 'Inclusion Isn't "Being Asked to Dance"'. *LinkedIn,* 3 May 2017. Available at: https://www.linkedin.com/pulse/inclusion-isnt-being-asked-dance-daniel-juday.

Kelly, D.J., Quinn, P.C., Slater, A.M., Lee, K. Gibson, A., Smith, M., Ge, L. and Pascalis, O. (2005) 'Three-Month-Olds, But Not Newborns, Prefer Own-Race Faces'. *Developmental Sciences,* 8(6): 31–36. Available at: https://www.ncbi.nlm.nih.gov/pmc/articles/PMC2566511/.

Lane, J. (2008) *Young Children and Racial Justice.* London: National Children's Bureau.

Lopez, G. (2016) 'Why You Should Stop Saying "All Lives Matter," Explained in 9 Different Ways'. *Vox,* 11 July 2016. Available at: https://www.vox.com/2016/7/11/12136140/black-all-lives-matter.

Louis, S. (2020) 'Let's Talk About Race'. *Nursery World,* 28 July 2020, pp. 16–17.

McIntosh, P. (1989) 'White Privilege: Unpacking the Invisible Knapsack'. *Peace and Freedom Magazine,* July/August 1989, pp. 10–12. Republished by *The SEED Project.* Available at: https://nationalseedproject.org/key-seed-texts/white-privilege-unpacking-the-invisible-knapsack.

Monmouth University (2020) 'Partisanship Drives Latest Shift in Race Relations Attitudes'. *Monmouth University*, July 8 2020. Available at: https://www.monmouth.edu/polling-institute/reports/monmouthpoll_us_070820/.

Mosby Tyler, D. (2020) 'Want a More Just World? Be an Unlikely Ally | Dwinita Mosby Tyler'. *YouTube*, 12 August 2020. Available at: https://youtu.be/Ruf6OdDRJSs?si=cgYgNne7Wm296nCD.

Office for National Statistics (2020) *Coronavirus (COVID-19) Related Deaths by Ethnic Group, England and Wales: 2 March 2020 to 10 April 2020*. Available at: https://www.ons.gov.uk/peoplepopulationandcommunity/birthsdeathsandmarriages/deaths/articles/coronavirusrelateddeathsbyethnicgroupenglandandwales/2march2020to10april2020.

Olusoga, D. (2020) 'Britain Is Not America. But We Too Are Disfigured by Deep and Pervasive Racism'. *The Guardian*, 7 June 2020. Available at: https://www.theguardian.com/commentisfree/2020/jun/07/britain-is-not-america-but-we-too-are-disfigured-by-deep-and-pervasive-racism.

Oxford English Dictionary Online (2023) "Ethnic Minority (N.)". Available at: https://doi.org/10.1093/OED/3042237841.

Shelter (2021) *Denied the Right to a Safe Home: Exposing the Housing Emergency*. Available at: https://assets.ctfassets.net/6sxvmndnpn0s/13hLYmEooTpZ79D9bxc57m/93869b373080f699b4b646300378f698/Shelter_Denied_the_right_to_a_safe_home_Report.pdf.

Sue, D.W., Capodilupo, C.M., Torino, G.C., Bucceri, J.M., Holder, A.M.B., Nadal, K.L. and Esquilin, M. (2007) 'Racial Microaggressions in Everyday Life: Implications for Clinical Practice'. *American Psychologist*, 62, pp. 271–286.

Tell MAMA (2018) *Normalising Hatred: Tell MAMA Annual Report 2018*. Available at: https://tellmamauk.org/wp-content/uploads/2019/09/Tell%20MAMA%20Annual%20Report%202018%20_%20Normalising%20Hate.pdf.

Tereshchenko, A., Mills, M. and Bradbury, A. (2020) *Making Progress? Employment and Retention of BAME Teachers in England*. London: UCL Institute of Education. Available at: https://discovery.ucl.ac.uk/id/eprint/10117331/1/IOE_Report_BAME_Teachers.pdf.

Tommy's (2022) *Tommy's Welcomes Black Maternity Experience Reports*. Available at: https://www.tommys.org/about-us/news-views/tommys-welcomes-black-maternity-experience-reports.

Toye, R. (2011) *Churchill's Empire: The World That Made Him and the World He Made*. London: Pan Macmillan.

Trade Union Congress (2022) *Still Rigged: Racism in the UK Labour Market 2022*. Available at: https://www.tuc.org.uk/sites/default/files/2022-08/RacismintheUKlabourmarket.pdf.

United States Sentencing Commission (2017) *Demographic Differences in Sentencing: An Update to the 2012 Booker Report*. Washington: United States Sentencing Commission. Available at: https://www.ussc.gov/sites/default/files/pdf/research-and-publications/research-publications/2017/20171114_Demographics.pdf.

Vollans, C. (2017) 'A Unique Child: Inclusion – Here's the Rub'. *Nursery World*, 20 February 2017. Available at: https://www.nurseryworld.co.uk/features/article/a-unique-child-inclusion-here-s-the-rub.

Women and Equalities Committee (2023) *Black Maternal Health: Third Report of Session 2022–23. HC 94*. London: House of Commons. Available at: https://committees.parliament.uk/publications/38989/documents/191706/default/.

Woodcock, A. (2020) 'Black Lives Matter: Boris Johnson Says UK "Not a Racist Country"'. *Independent*, 8 June 2020. Available at: https://www.independent.co.uk/news/uk/politics/boris-johnson-uk-racist-country-black-lives-matter-protests-colston-a9554356.html.

Xiao, N.G., Quinn, P.C., Liu, S., Ge, L., Pascalis, O. and Lee, K. (2017) 'Older But Not Younger Infants Associated Own-Race Faces with Happy Music and Other-Race Faces with Sad Music'. *Developmental Science*, 3 February 2017. Available at: https://onlinelibrary.wiley.com/doi/10.1111/desc.12537

Ye Hee Lee, M. (2015) 'Donald Trump's False Comments Connecting Mexican Immigrants and Crime'. *The Washington Post*, 8 July 2015. Available at: https://www.washingtonpost.com/news/fact-checker/wp/2015/07/08/donald-trumps-false-comments-connecting-mexican-immigrants-and-crime/.

YMCA (2020) *Young and Black: The Young Black Experience of Institutional Racism in the UK*. Available at: https://www.ymca.org.uk/wp-content/uploads/2020/10/ymca-young-and-black.pdf.

Part 1

Equity and practice
How to break the cycle

2

Unravelling bias

Stella Louis and Hannah Betteridge

Observation is the cornerstone of effective early years practice. It requires patience, empathy, self-control, and a significant knowledge of child development to accurately inform our assessment of what stage a child is at. Using this information, you can create an environment that effectively supports children's learning through well-designed activities that are challenging and engaging and tailored to the unique needs of the child.

Observations, however, are not facts. They are highly subjective and are based purely on our *perception* of what we have seen. Depending on what you think is significant and what you are looking for, you may notice different things or interpret the same behaviour differently to another educator. Let's take two-year-old Ruben as an example. One day, Ruben was observed repeatedly emptying a box of pencils all over the floor. After several attempts to clear up the mess that Ruben has made, you watch him deliberately scatter the pencils on the floor again. In this scenario, what would be your assessment of Ruben's behaviour?

Some may view his behaviour as disruptive or naughty and actively discourage it – after all, he is creating a trip hazard for the other children in the setting. Others, with a knowledge of schematic development, may spot that Ruben has a scattering schema and therefore go on to identify safe ways to support his knowledge and understanding of space and quantities by providing him with meaningful opportunities to spread toys around the room in different ways.[1]

What we see when we observe children ultimately affects what we do. That is why as educators, we must continually reflect on whether we are *truly* seeing what is in front of us, or whether we only see what we *want* or are *conditioned* to see. If we are unaware of how bias and stereotypes filter the lens through which we see the world, we can unwittingly restrict the learning opportunities we offer to children and make poor judgements about their development and learning. This can have a hugely detrimental impact

DOI: 10.4324/9781003251149-3

on a child's confidence and their educational attainment at an early age. For Black children in particular, the effects of educator bias have been proven to be incredibly damaging for decades (Coard, 2021). In order to ensure that we can effectively provide *every* child we teach with meaningful learning experiences, we must critically reflect on our observations and the decisions we make through the assessment and planning process, with active consideration given to how we identify and address our own personal biases.

Unconscious bias

We all make instinctive judgements based on the things that we see, feel, and hear. We do this consciously or unconsciously as a result of experiences we have had, things we have been told, or messages we have unwittingly absorbed. This is a normal and unavoidable part of being human. It affects us all.

On a daily basis, our brains are constantly bombarded with information; literally billions of stimuli that we have to rapidly sort and interpret for our survival, but we can't possibly process it all. In fact, neuroscientists have shown that of the 11 million pieces of information we take in every second, we only have the capacity to consciously process about 40 of them (Fan, 2014). To save time and effort, our brain makes shortcuts using the way we have been socialised, our memories, and our knowledge to inform our thoughts, words, and actions. This process happens automatically, often without thinking, and often not on the basis of the evidence we have in front of us at the time.

Even if we don't believe what we have heard about a person or group on a conscious level, in making the snap and automatic decisions that are necessary for our survival, our brain relies on the information and codes we have absorbed from our environment in the past. The problem is, if we have grown up in a society and environment that places primacy on Whiteness, that tells us one race is a model minority whilst another is a problem minority, this bleeds into our behaviour. This unconscious bias influences our decision-making, our attitudes, our preferences, and the beliefs we hold. It leads us to put disproportionate weight for or against a person, idea, group, or thing without reason or just cause. It can stop us from seeing what is truly there.

Whether you want to hear it or not, the reality is: you are biased. We are all biased. This fact may make you feel profoundly uncomfortable, embarrassed, guilty, or ashamed. But it shouldn't. Being biased doesn't automatically make you a bad person and it doesn't make you racist; it simply makes you human.

The issue comes not in being biased, but when we are unaware or unwilling to accept, acknowledge, and mitigate our bias. Studies into academic attainment, socioeconomic outcomes, health inequalities, and the criminal justice system show time after time that '[f]ailing to recognise or address our bias can have catastrophic results at an individual and societal level. It entrenches prejudice. It entrenches inequality' (Louis and Betteridge, 2020a). Shying away from acknowledging or discussing our bias may eliminate the awkwardness we feel, but it won't address the pain and inequality that others experience. The only thing that will do that is conscious, sustained, and meaningful action.

Stereotypes

Stereotypes are sweeping statements, overgeneralisations, or categorisations that we make about a particular group based on their gender, race, ethnicity, background, or class. They are based on perception, not on reality. Two stereotypes we hear a lot in Western cultures are that Black males are defiant and challenging and that Black females are sassy and aggressive. Even though it is statistically impossible that every single person within one race will have the exact same defining personality trait, stereotypes continue to hold weight, affecting our decision-making abilities and our behaviour. The stereotype that all Black boys are aggressive, for example, trickles into perceptions of criminality, leading to the over-policing of Black neighbourhoods and the greater use of force by the police against Black residents when compared to their White counterparts (Weir, 2016).

Young children are not immune from these effects. In 2014, the United States Department of Education reported that despite only making up 18% of all American preschoolers, Black children accounted for 42% of all preschool suspensions. When *The New York Times* ran this story, some of its readers argued that the disparity could be explained by the fact that 'minority children committed more serious offences' (Staples, 2014). The kicker? Investigations into these disparities 'routinely turn up evidence of school districts invoking harsher punishments against minority students than their non-minority classmates, even when the behaviours being punished are identical' (Staples, 2014). The problem then is clearly not the behaviour that Black children exhibit, it is the way that we perceive it. By presenting incomplete sweeping statements as the single version of the truth, stereotypes 'make one story become the only story' (Adichie, 2016). Every child and every adult of every race has the potential to be defiant, sassy, or aggressive. Just because we meet one person who displays one of those traits does not mean that everyone in the same racial group will display the same behaviour.

Not all racial stereotypes are disparaging. However, this does not make them any less damaging, or any less racist. For example, you may have heard the notion that Asian children are extremely intelligent and particularly good at maths. This stereotype may seem innocuous at first because of its seemingly complimentary nature. Yet, as an educator, internalising this view could significantly curtail your ability to see a child's full talents and abilities; it may lead you to push a child away from more creative pursuits or prevent you from seeing the academic abilities of others simply because you don't expect them to be there.

Just like unconscious bias, stereotypical beliefs can therefore influence how we observe, assess, and plan for children, as well as the opportunities we offer them to support their development and learning. They can also affect the judgements we make about their families and the support we extend to them. When left unexamined, they may result in incorrect assessments, leading to a learning environment and interactions that do not meet a child's individual needs. This can have a devastating effect on their

- Individual development, including their personal, social, and emotional development.
- Individual interests.
- Communication style.
- Learning preferences.

Where do stereotypes and unconscious bias come from?

Our beliefs and attitudes are learnt early in childhood and deeply ingrained. Throughout our lives, we are repeatedly exposed to other people's perceptions and assumptions, from our parents, grandparents, and peers, in books, on television, and in the media. Little by little, these interfere with our perception of reality. We may have to search very deeply for the reason why we feel what we feel, or perceive what we perceive, and how this affects the way that we interact with, acknowledge, and respond to other people and their children, especially those who are from a different cultural background to ourselves.

Most of us would vigorously deny that inequality or prejudice were present in our practice, even if unconsciously. However, unless we are prepared to routinely reflect on the decisions that we make, as well as examine our beliefs and tendencies to stereotype, then we cannot know with any certainty how our prejudgements and assumptions about children affect our attitudes, practice, and provision (National Strategies, 2009). As Fiarman (2019) argues,

> you may not be waking up in the morning with a desire to treat black kids unfairly, but you are waking up in the morning in a society that is indoctrinating you daily to believe that white is normal, and anything else is other, and often less than.

Exercise

The following visualisation exercise will help to challenge and support you in understanding the impact that your bias, beliefs, and attitudes can have on young children and their families.

Take a piece of paper and imagine the following three scenarios. Visualise:

- A child that is overachieving.
- A child that is solitary, quiet, and reflective.
- A child that is cooperative and well-behaved.

Write down what you see.

Was the overachieving child Black? Was the solitary, quiet and reflective child mixed-race? Was the cooperative and well-behaved child Roma? It is fine if one or all of your answers are no, but we would encourage you to reflect on why.

Here are some questions that you might want to think about:

- Do you reward, punish, or give the benefit of the doubt to the actions and behaviours you see consistently across different groups of children?

35

- Do the highest-achieving children in your setting usually share the same background, race, or ethnicity?
- Do you expect certain children or groups of children to have particular communication styles – e.g., quiet or argumentative?
- Imagine you had to write a pros and cons list to support your assessment. What evidence objectively supports your view that Child A is smart and well-behaved, whilst Child B is naughty? Do other staff in your setting, perhaps those of a different background to yourself, share the same view? Why or why not?
- How do you know that your observation and assessment practices are accurate and free from stereotypical influences?
- How frequently do you reflect on your personal attitudes, practices, behaviours, and the impact that these have on others?

We often attribute greater worth to individuals who are like us. This is because our brains create images of things that we are used to seeing and these things become normal, desirable, and familiar. Whereas things that are unfamiliar become less desirable or more likely to be perceived as untrue. As a result, our unconscious bias develops from the thoughts and familiar images that we consume. When left unchecked, our unconscious bias can reinforce problematic beliefs about race. The more we draw on them or perceive them, the more likely it is that they will become an entrenched part of our core beliefs, creating a vicious cycle and thereby increasing the likelihood of discriminatory practice.

Why do they matter?

Whilst we're busy observing and assessing the children that we care for, it can be all too easy to overlook ourselves. Yet our thoughts, words, and actions have the power to dramatically shape a child's view of themselves and the world around them, for the better but also for the worse. As educators, we are placed in a position of trust and power – with an explicit expectation that we will act in the best interests of the child and support their development. We cannot do this effectively without critically examining our own values, being honest with ourselves about our biases, and committing to actively challenge ourselves and others. Failure to do this puts us at serious risk of ignoring the unique voice of the child and ultimately failing to adequately support their needs.

In their review of the effect of bias on teachers' behaviour, Gilliam *et al.* (2016: 3) noted that '[t]here is evidence that empathic responses are dampened when the observer is of a different race than the observed, suggesting that teachers may be less likely to respond with empathy when a child of a race different to her own is exhibiting challenging behaviours'. The effects of this are hugely significant, not least when you consider that the vast majority of the early years workforce is White (Department for Education, 2021). Indeed, through their study, Gilliam *et al.* (2016) concluded that when primed to expect challenging behaviour, teachers gazed longer at Black children, especially Black boys, despite no behavioural challenges actually being present in the videos they were asked to observe.

As educators begin to gain awareness and become more knowledgeable about the different and diverse cultural practices of the children attending the setting, their tendency to make stereotypical judgements greatly reduces, and they are more equipped to call out and challenge stereotypes and bias when they see it. It is therefore important that all educators develop their practice to ensure that close examination of their attitudes and behaviours is built into their approach on a regular basis. As part of this, educators should consider who they are and how this influences their practice.

Continuous professional development is an important tool to encourage educators to engage in deep, meaningful discussion to reduce racial disparities, whilst also helping them to become more aware of their conscious and unconscious beliefs and how these affect their teaching. In order to develop their practice, educators need to challenge negative attitudes and talk openly and honestly about issues of equality, equity, diversity, and inclusion within their setting. Chamberlain (2016: 20) suggests: 'To know the true reality of yourself, you must be aware not only of your conscious thoughts, but also of your unconscious prejudices, bias and habits'. Educators will need to come together to think carefully about other people's perspectives and the voice of the child. This means, as an individual and as a team, reflecting on what is meant by prejudice and discrimination and how this is played out in practice, attitudes, and behaviours. When educators recognise their own bias and use of stereotypes in their behaviour, they are in a better position to begin to minimise it and prevent themselves from acting instinctively. Discussions about discriminatory behaviour are important because they tend to highlight conscious and unconscious practices that disadvantage and discriminate against particular groups of children and their families.

Being able to carry out bias-free observations of children's relationships, needs, development, and learning is a central part of effective pedological practice. If educators allow their biases to affect the decisions that they make about a child's development, this may lead to inappropriate activities and expectations. Unconscious bias can occur at any stage of the observation, assessment, and planning process, affecting the practitioner's understanding and interpretation of what they have seen. When these unconscious biases interfere with this process, subsequent assessment and planning are out of tune with the child. It is interesting to note that age, race, education, and gender are often identified as biases in observation by educators.

Affinity bias

Affinity bias refers to gravitating towards someone because they are similar to you, maybe you have a similar physical appearance to them, share similar experiences with them, or have similar interests and/or cultural practices. It is about preferring or being more comfortable with people who look like or think and act like you. As a result, we move away from or reject people who we perceive to be less like us. The following case study illustrates the negative impact that affinity bias can have if it is not examined and countered in educational settings.

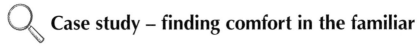 ## Case study – finding comfort in the familiar

Tamara is the key worker for Joe and Ezra, both of whom are two years old. Joe and Tamara are White and Ezra is Black. Tamara has been overheard frequently saying that Joe reminds her of her grown-up son when he was that age. All morning Ezra had been playing in the block area, repeatedly building vertical towers until they fell down. Joe came into the block area and deliberately knocked Ezra's tower over. Ezra shouted 'No' at Joe, and Joe moved away. A short time later, he returned and again pushed Ezra's tower over. This time, Ezra pushed him away. Joe fell and began to cry. Having not witnessed the full interaction, Tamara approached the block area and asked Joe what had happened. He told Tamara that Ezra pushed him. Without asking Ezra what happened, Tamara demanded that Ezra apologise to Joe and find somewhere else to play. Joe's behaviour towards Ezra was not addressed.

Tamara's decision to only focus her attention on Joe and to overlook Ezra was based on the affinity she had with Joe. Moreover, her tendency to favour Joe, because he reminds her of her son, led her to unwittingly discriminate against Ezra. Ezra was completely left out of the conversation about what had taken place; his voice, views, and experience were ignored. Pratt-Harris *et al.* (2016) note that the unconscious feelings we have towards other people 'play a strong part in influencing our judgements of certain people and groups, away from being balanced or even-handed, in many different areas of life'. As a result, it is vital that educators are aware of the affinity that they have with children and families so that they can think about the effect that their interactions and behaviours have on them. The danger with affinity bias is that it influences our interactions and decisions. It can leave groups of children feeling like they are on the outside.

Confirmation bias

Confirmation bias refers to how we search for, interpret, and recall information looking for things that validate or affirm the way that we already see someone, even in the face of overwhelming evidence to the contrary. When observing a child, we may see specific information or evidence that confirms our assumptions and quickly dismiss or minimise anything that suggests the contrary. We therefore give a lot more weight to evidence that supports our beliefs. Confirmation bias, like affinity bias, is powerful and we need to take it into account when observing and evaluating children's development and learning.

Case study – proving what I already know

Emmanuel, a five-year-old Black boy of Jamaican heritage, attended the reception class of a small primary school in South London. Emma, the teacher of the class, shared her observations of Emmanuel with Pam, the teaching assistant. Emma told Pam that Emmanuel was a difficult boy who frequently misbehaved and whom she struggled to understand. She described one encounter with Emmanuel where he was very reluctant to take part in writing activities that she had set for the group. Instead, he insisted on going outside to play, so she had just ignored him all morning. As a result of his behavioural issues, Emma thought it was likely that Emmanuel would fail to reach the expected standard of development by the time he left reception.

Pam disagreed and told Emma that Emmanuel came into reception able to write his own name and simple sentences. She recalled him writing a simple story for her about how when he grew up he was not going to crack his phone, after she had told the children that she had dropped and cracked her own phone. Emma looked surprised but dismissed Pam's comments, suggesting that she had been mistaken. 'It must have been another child', Emma replied. As a result, Emma failed to support Emmanuel's desire to write his own stories effectively because of her confirmation bias.

According to Ina Catrinescu,

> [c]onfirmation bias is our most treasured enemy. Our opinions, our acumen – all of it, are the result of years of selectively choosing to pay attention to that information only which confirms what our limited minds already accept as truth.
>
> (as quoted in Yaafouri, 2018)

It is easy to see how this plays out in the case study above. In her discussions about Emmanuel's behaviour, Emma drew conclusions, assuming he was naughty and underachieving, even in the face of evidence to the contrary, rather than thinking about how she could have made the exercise more engaging for him to extend his learning. To effectively support the unique needs of the child, it is fundamental that educators are able to recognise children's achievements and use their interests and ideas to stimulate and take learning forward in meaningful ways. That involves bringing the curriculum to children, rather than expecting them to fit into the curriculum. For example, if we know a child enjoys playing outside and finds it harder to concentrate indoors, we can create more favourable conditions for learning by providing opportunities outside for mark making, or in the case above, provide opportunities for children to write about things that they are already interested in.

If we only draw on information that aligns with our views, values, and beliefs about individual children, we cannot hope to objectively assess the development of the child. This lack of objectivity can lead to inappropriate decisions being made about children's development and learning, which is why it is so important to have time to reflect on observations and interpretations.

The halo and horn effect

The halo effect (sometimes referred to as the halo error) is when we believe that a child can do no wrong because they have a particular characteristic or trait that we view positively. These characteristics can include someone's physical attributes (e.g., their race), or their religion, culture, language, or accent. When the halo effect is at play, it can lead us to assume that the children we teach with traits that we like are more likely to succeed academically, are better behaved, and are more trustworthy, without any objective evidence to back up our views. In making these assumptions, we end up unconsciously treating certain groups more favourably than others, choosing to invest more time in their development and creating a self-fulfilling prophecy.

The reverse is also true. When a child has a characteristic or trait that we dislike, we are more predisposed to think negatively about everything else that they do; this is called the 'horn effect'. We may therefore be more likely to enact stricter punishments on different groups of children displaying the same behaviour based on our assessment of whether we think they are 'good' or 'bad'. Ultimately, the halo and horn effect 'inclines us to match our view of all the qualities of a person to our judgement of one attribute that is particularly significant' (Kahneman, 2011: 199). The trouble is that this not only encourages us to respond to the same behaviour differently according to who displays it, but it also prevents us from questioning why we *perceive* some children to be 'good' and others to be 'bad'.

 # Case study – silent treatment

Adapted from Louis, S. and Betteridge, H. (2020b) *Unconscious Bias in the Observation, Assessment and Planning Process*. Foundation Stage Forum.

After reading the reception class a story, the teacher, Annette, asked the group questions about it. Several White boys shouted out the answers and were encouraged to participate further and share their ideas as the discussion continued. Romeo, a Black boy, then called out an answer. Annette directed him to put his hand up if he wanted to say something and told him to stop being disruptive, despite encouraging the White children to participate earlier. After several attempts to get Annette's attention by putting his hand up and being deliberately ignored by her, Romeo disengaged from the discussion altogether. The next day, Romeo continued to disengage from story time. His parents noticed a difference in his behaviour at home.

This example shows how the horn effect can silence children and prevent them from expressing themselves and sharing their knowledge, whilst the halo effect can reward the same behaviour from others. When educators have such biases, they make it difficult for children to be seen or heard. The limitation of an educator's expectations can shut children down. As we can see here, children may become disengaged and less likely to share their insights or ask questions because they quickly come to learn that they will not be chosen. If children feel unappreciated, or like the educator does not understand them, they are more likely to retreat inwards or act out in other ways to elicit attention. Every educator has a responsibility to respect and value children's ideas and contributions irrespective of their race, ethnicity, religion, or culture. However, as Cullen Hightower argues, '[i]t's hard to see a halo when you're looking for horns' (Hightower as quoted in Pearce, 1996).

The implications this can have on a child's receptiveness to learn, and their future achievements can be profound. Educators make hundreds of decisions about children's learning during the day. Without being able to objectively assess the stage of development that children are at, we can overlook children's actual performance and miss opportunities for learning.

Attribution bias

Attribution bias refers to the systemic errors that we make when we try to find reasons to justify our own actions, behaviours, and motivations, as well as the actions, behaviours, and motivations of children and their families based on their character or personality. This often leads us to ignore or minimise the impact of situational or environmental factors at play, even when they are otherwise obvious. Attribution bias can affect how we evaluate, respond, interact with, and treat children and their families as a result. To counteract attribution bias, it is important that we look beyond the assumptions that we have made about a child's moral character and instead keep an open mind, looking at the context in which the situation has occurred. As Psychologist Lee Ross points out: 'the error lies in our inclination to attribute people's behaviour to *the way they are*, rather than the situation they are in' (1977).

Case study – running around tables

Toby is the teacher of a reception class. He teaches children aged between four and five years old. One morning, he directed the girls from his class to run around inside. When the girls had finished, Toby then instructed the boys to do the same. Femi, who is Black, had been on time out for 45 minutes for talking during reading time before he was asked to join the boys. As Femi ran around the table for the second time, he accidentally bumped into some of the boys who had slowed down, resulting in one boy falling over and Femi falling onto a chair and hurting himself. Toby shouted at Femi as he cried, accusing him of being too aggressive. The accident was blamed on what Toby saw as Femi's inherent personality traits of being disruptive, rather than considering that Femi may have had more energy to burn having been on time out for 45 minutes or that he was simply so absorbed by the task at hand that he wasn't paying attention to the space around him. Femi's motivations were viewed through the lens of aggression.

The danger with attribution bias is that it does not consider the context, or indeed any contributing factors. Instead, it focuses on the child's assumed character and underestimates the context in which the situation occurred. Indeed, in this example, Toby's attribution bias prevented him from ensuring that he reprimanded Femi fairly, acknowledging that he was hurt and comforting him appropriately.

Observing young children with equity

In Western societies, educational attainment data has highlighted the chronic underachievement of Black boys, particularly Black Caribbean students, at every stage of the educational system for some time (Demie and Mclean, 2017). Teacher expectations are arguably one of the key drivers behind such outcomes. In one now-famous experiment, which was conducted in San Francisco by Rosenthal and Jacobson in the 1960s, children were asked to complete IQ tests at the start of the school year. Their teachers were then told which children were the most intelligent. However, rather than telling the teachers which children actually scored highest on the IQ tests, Rosenthal and Jacobson picked 20 names at random and told the teachers that these children were the smartest, even though they were not. At the end of the school year, the children were asked to complete IQ tests again. Interestingly, the study found that the children the teachers were told were the smartest outperformed all the other children in the IQ test by quite significant margins. For first graders (six- and seven-year-olds), the difference between those that the teachers believed were the brightest and those they did not was, on average, 15.5 points. When interviewed about their classes, the teachers described the children from whom intellectual growth was expected as being 'happier, more curious, and more interesting than the other children' (Rosenthal and Jacobson, 1968). By contrast, the children who demonstrated an improvement between their first and second IQ test were rated less favourably by their teachers if their teachers had not expected them to do well. In fact, the more they gained, the less favourably they were rated by their teachers.

Rosenthal and Jacobson's study clearly shows the impact that teachers' beliefs and expectations can have on the academic attainment of their pupils. It highlighted that even subtle behaviours, like our tone of voice, can communicate our expectations of pupils, creating more positive conditions for learning for those that we believe in. If you consider the percentage point difference between the two groups of children – those who were believed to have the propensity to excel academically and those who were not – it is easy to see the life-changing effects that a teacher's beliefs can have on a child's outcomes.

The disparities we see in educational attainment, particularly amongst Black boys, tend to translate into higher rates of unemployment and a steep pay gap in comparison to their White counterparts as they progress into adult life. The reasons for this are complex and there is no simple solution. Socioeconomic factors and the role that parents play at home can definitely have an impact. However, '[m]ost studies report that controls for socio-economic status typically reduce the Black-White gap by no more than one-third, and often by less, and that substantial gaps remain' (Strand, 2012). With two-thirds of the attainment gap unexplained by socioeconomic factors alone, it is clear that we need to consider the role that educators play.

Often the role of educators and the pervasiveness of bias, prejudice, and discrimination at an individual and structural level is ignored or overlooked; partly because discussing race is still seen to be so taboo that it silences progress, and partly because it can be easier to deflect the cause of racial disparities onto other factors, rather than accept responsibility and the role we can play in perpetuating or challenging outcomes. Indeed, according to Professor Feysia Demie, 'four main schools-related factors have emerged [as causes of underachievement amongst Black children]: stereotyping; teachers' low expectations; exclusions; and headteachers' poor leadership on equality issues' (2003: 243). These factors, which result in less favourable attitudes and beliefs being projected onto Black children, are then often internalised by students, who to start to believe that they are unintelligent or disengage from the system altogether. If you are repeatedly told that you have reached the limit of what you can achieve by those in positions of power, it is not surprising that you start to believe it.

Developing your practice

In assessing children's development, it is essential that educators strive to critically reflect on their observations, regularly inviting the views of others, to protect their assessments from bias and stereotyping. The observation, assessment, and planning process should not be a solo endeavour. It should include taking part in regular discussions about a child's progress in which you reflect on the meaning of their actions and words and at the same time create a learning environment that supports and challenges them.

As an educator, you should not underestimate the impact you have on the lives of the babies and young children that you work with. The Effective Provision for Preschool Education (EPPE) Project, which was a longitudinal study conducted by Sylva *et al.* (2004), found that educators have a signifi-cant impact on children's learning. In the study, children's attitudes and moti-vation to learn were directly influenced by the interaction and feedback that they received from educators. Given the sizeable impact that interactions and behaviour can have, all educators have a moral and ethical responsibility to reflect on their attitudes, behaviours, practice, and pedagogy.

As Froebel highlights,

> [w]hen assumptions about children's attitudes are drawn from their behaviour, then widespread mistakes can be made. The child who seems rude and self-willed is often involved in an intense struggle to realise the good by [their] own effort.
>
> (Froebel, as quoted in Lilley, 1967: 51)

To prevent educators filling in the gaps with their preconceptions, it is impor-tant that they build relationships with children before they observe them. These relationships should be close, trusting, responsive, interactive, and

45

intellectually engaging. Learning about children's play experiences, position in the family, likes and dislikes, strengths, interests, and motivation will help the educator understand the child as a whole person and should inform the approach to curriculum planning. Fundamentally, observation is about trying to understand the child and when educators build trusting relationships with children, they are better able to tune into the child's needs in a meaningful way that seeks to build on the child's prior experiences.

It is important that educators give all children the benefit of the doubt, rather than fostering a deficit approach. Our observations should build on the positive characteristics of each individual child, supporting and extending what they can already do, rather than what they are not yet able to do. Nursery settings and schools should be democratic, respectful communities of learners, where adults and children can learn from each other. They should be closely connected to the wider learning community of people and places.

Educators should also strive to consider how they can create a more equitable approach to observing children. This means taking into account children's unique and diverse experiences; otherwise, discriminatory and biased practices will continue to exist. It may not always be possible to capture all of a child's progression through predefined curriculum statements. A diverse and inclusive approach to observation would look for other ways to capture observable progression. For example, staff at a London nursery school recently undertook training on the stages of English Language Acquisition (a UK-based framework for assessing language skills), as they had a number of attending children with English as a second language. Children's progress at the nursery was regularly monitored and staff acted upon the findings. They found that children with English as a second language were not making the level of progress expected. The framework provided participants with specific information about young children's linguistic development. Participants were encouraged to closely observe how the child used their home language as they played and interacted with others. During the training, participants were asked to reflect on their responses and expectations. They realised that they were focusing on the fact that these children could not speak English, rather than what they were capable of understanding. The training gave them the confidence to capture other observable behaviours, such as the children's concentration, their development of control in using functional language in their play, and the non-verbal gestures they used to help clarify meaning. It enabled the participants to better meet the needs of children with English as a second language because they had a better understanding of the child's linguistic needs and development. This new knowledge empowered them to broaden the learning experiences and reduce their interventions.

To provide balance and minimise the chance that bias takes hold, schools and settings should have strategies in place that ensure the same person does not observe the same child all the time. Instead, at regular intervals, a group of staff could observe, interpret, enquire, and learn about the child as a team, reflecting on what has been discovered about the child and about themselves as observers. These strategies help educators to align their observations, focusing only on what they have seen and not what they want to see. For Froebel, observing without reflection was 'empty observation' which could never lead to real understanding (as quoted in Liebschner, 1992: 141). Reflecting on how diverse and inclusive your observational processes are can therefore be seen to be an essential part of a practitioner's pedagogical practice, as well as being a vital building block of equitable practice.

Reflective questions

- Which forms of bias have you witnessed taking place in your setting?
- Next time you notice bias at play, what could you do differently to prevent it from skewing the lens through which a child in your care is seen?

Fostering an anti-bias approach to observation, assessment, and planning

Fostering an anti-bias approach is not just about acknowledging and understanding that children are unique; it's about being committed to critically examining how our thought structures affect our decisions and our behaviours, to ensure that we are not unconsciously sabotaging a child's chances on the basis of their race, culture, ethnicity, religion, or background. Educators need to interrupt and break down the cycle of bias and stereotyping that can have a harmful impact on relationships with children, our expectations of them, and, ultimately, their development, learning, and progression.

Step one: acceptance

Breaking the cycle of bias and stereotypes clouding our judgements is a life-long process that requires sustained and conscious effort. You will make mistakes along the way, and you won't always get it right. But like we tell the children we teach, we can't let our fear of making mistakes keep us from trying. We have to keep going, leaning into our discomfort along the way to do better next time. No matter how much you read, study, or talk about race, there will always be more to learn. We can always know better and do better.

Step two: changing the rules

The current system is not working. It serves some children, whilst underestimating others for no other reason than the colour of their skin. Whilst we can't stop being biased, we can reduce the impact it has on our attitudes and behaviours. To do this, we have to scrutinise the context of our decision-making at an individual level by:

- Carrying out regular analysis of children's progress to ensure that all children have fair and equitable access to early education.
- Looking for evidence that counters our views and actively seeking out other viewpoints – for example, by asking a child's family or carer about their behaviour at home or gathering views from other educators in your setting.
- Guarding against jumping to conclusions – for example, seeing a child demonstrate one negative or positive behaviour and assuming that means a child is 'good' or 'bad', 'smart' or 'underachieving' – by ensuring your observations take place over time and involve self-reflection.
- Asking ourselves whether our thoughts are linked to factual evidence about what is known about the child, or our preconceptions.
- Questioning whether we would handle a particular situation differently if this child or parent looked like me or didn't look like me.

By scrutinising our decisions in this way, we can open ourselves to different possibilities.

Another vital part of this process is considering the impact of the structures around us. Attention should be paid to the creation of an inclusive physical and emotional learning environment, the individual needs of the child, and representations of diversity within the setting. (These concepts are explored more in Chapters 4 and 5.) As an educator, you are responsible for creating the right conditions for learning. This includes providing opportunities and experiences for different learning styles and incorporating themes that interest children and meet their needs. For example, in one setting we observed a four-year-old Black boy being asked to write his name on his painting by his teacher. He replied, 'No, I don't want to… I don't want to, but can I draw a spaceship'. Rather than focusing on his refusal to write his name, his teacher gave him the opportunity to paint a spaceship, which he later named, writing both his name and the name of the spaceship on the paper. By creating a learning environment in which children are given opportunities to develop their self-esteem, self-worth, and self-confidence, the teacher gave this child what he needed to thrive. To achieve this, educators need to be genuinely interested in observing and getting to know the children they teach. Giving children choices about what and where they play can also provide children with a sense of control which in turn helps to develop their confidence.

Educators should strive to acknowledge and understand the assessment inequities that exist and the impact that these have on children's development, learning, and outcomes. However, this will take work as educators may not instantly recognise these inequalities or understand their impact if they are not conscious of their own internal bias. Educators will need to take personal responsibility for their own behaviour and actions influenced by bias and work towards eliminating it.

Reflective questions

Take a moment to consider the following:

- What policies and processes do you have in place to promote equity, diversity, and inclusion within your setting?
- Are you encouraged to take a deficit or asset-based approach to observation, assessment, and planning?
- In your setting, does all planning start with observation?
- Do you use your observations to help you focus on how you could structure the learning environment to engage children who appear reluctant to participate in particular activities, whilst showing high levels of involvement in others?

- Do you regularly consult with children and their families about what further resources they would like to see within the setting?
- How do you actively create an environment where children feel safe and comfortable in their own skin?
- What are the issues and concerns for children from different ethnicities in your school or setting? How do you know? How have you responded to or addressed these issues?

Step three: be the change you want to see in the world

You should embed discussions about equity, diversity, and inclusion within your team, role model positive behaviours by taking responsibility for biased decisions and interactions, and consciously work to address any issues you have identified in your practice or attitudes through reading this book. As part of any discussions you have about race, it is important that you avoid shaming or humiliating people for their behaviour or actions; doing so is only likely to alienate people and make them more reluctant to engage in a dialogue about race in the future. Discussions should be constructive and supportive, seeking to focus on how we can do things differently next time, rather than making value judgements.

Examining our own attitudes, feelings, and preconceptions, and encouraging others to do the same can feel uncomfortable. However, unless we do this, we cannot say with any degree of certainty that we have given due consideration to how our attitudes, thoughts, and behaviours may affect our practice, pedagogy, and provision. It is vital that we create safe spaces for open and honest dialogue with our colleagues and get together to check that our observations and assessments are free of bias and assumptions. Together, you should review and reflect on the observations that you have gathered as a team. Look at how you are using them to gather information to support children. Are they negative or positive? What kind of supporting evidence do you provide? Can you see any patterns emerging for a specific race or gender, underachievement, or overachievement? What insights can you gather about best practice from the observations, assessments and plans that have been shared? How can you embed these within your practice, or support someone else to do the same?

Exercise

Repeat the exercise you conducted at the start of this chapter. Take a piece of paper and imagine the following three scenarios.
Visualise:

- A child that is overachieving.
- A child that is solitary, quiet, and reflective.
- A child that is cooperative and well-behaved.

Write down what you see.
Hopefully your visualisations are significantly different from your first ones.

There is an urgent need for educators to become more aware of and challenge our own unconscious biases during the observation, assessment, and planning process. Otherwise, children will continue to be unfairly and inaccurately assessed as under or overachieving because of the skin they were born in. The collective effect of our unconscious biases at an individual and structural level is extremely powerful. Whilst they may be normal, they form invisible barriers to children, acting as a straitjacket for progress and impeding growth and development, unless we choose to do something about them. They can cause us to do things that we do not mean to do, say things that we do not mean to say, and hurt the feelings of children and families without understanding how we have caused that hurt.

The care and education of young children are too essential to the future of our society for us to keep getting it wrong. Young children are entitled to knowledgeable and well-qualified professionals who are deeply informed about and attuned to the distinctive nature of young children's learning and development irrespective of their race, ethnicity, religion, or background. We owe it to the children we teach to reflect deeply on how we may react differently to some children than others.

Note

1 A schema is a repeated pattern of behaviour often observed within children's play. 'They link directly to the development and strengthening of cognitive structures in the brain' (Louis, 2016).

References

Adichie, C. (2016) *The Danger of a Single Story*. Available at: https://www.ted.com/talks/chimamanda_ngozi_adichie_the_danger_of_a_single_story.

Chamberlain, R. (2016) *Conscious Leadership in the Workplace: A Guidebook to Making a Difference*. New York: Morgan James Publishing.

Coard, B. (2021) *How the West Indian Child is Made Educationally Sub-Normal in the British School System*. Expanded 5th edn. Kingston: McDermott Publishing.

Department for Education (2021) *Survey of Childcare and Early Year Providers: Main Summary, England, 2021*. Available at: https://www.gov.uk/government/statistics/childcare-and-early-years-providers-survey-2021.

Demie, F. (2003) 'Raising the Achievement of Black Caribbean Pupils in British Schools: Unacknowledged Problems and Challenges for Policy Makers'. *London Review of Education*, 1(3), pp. 229–248.

Demie, F. and Mclean, C. (2017) *Black Caribbean Underachievement in Schools in England*. London: Schools Research and Statistics Unit.

Fan, J. (2014) 'An Information Theory Account of Cognitive Control'. *Frontiers in Human Neuroscience*. Available at: https://www.frontiersin.org/articles/10.3389/fnhum.2014.00680/full

Fiarman, S. (2019) as quoted in J. Anderson, 'Harvard EdCast: Unconscious Bias in Schools'. 20 November. Available at: https://www.gse.harvard.edu/news/19/11/harvard-edcast-unconscious-bias-schools.

Gilliam, W.S., Maupin, A.N., Reyes, C.R., Accavitti, M. and Shic, F. (2016) *Do Early Educators' Implicit Biases Regarding Sex and Race Relate to Behavior Expectations and Recommendations of Preschool Expulsions and Suspensions?* New Haven: Yale University Child Study Center.

Kahneman, D. (2011) *Thinking, Fast and Slow*. New York: Farrar, Straus and Giroux.

Liebschner, J. (1992) *A Child's Work: Freedom and Guidance in Froebel's Educational Theory and Practice*. Cambridge: Lutterworth Press.

Lilley, I.M. (1967) *Friedrich Froebel. A Selection from His Writings*. Cambridge: Cambridge University Press.

Louis, S. (2016) 'The Importance of Schemas in Every Child's Learning'. *Community Play Things*. Available at: https://www.communityplaythings.co.uk/learning-library/articles/schemas-by-stella-louis.

Louis, S. and Betteridge, H. (2020a) 'Let's Talk About Bias in the Early Years'. *Famly*. Available at: https://www.famly.co/blog/bias-in-early-years.

Louis, S. and Betteridge, H. (2020b) *Unconscious Bias in the Observation, Assessment and Planning Process*. Foundation Stage Forum. Available at: https://eyfs.info/articles.html/general/unconscious-bias-in-the-observation-assessment-and-planning-process-r338/.

National Strategies (2009) *'Building Futures: Believing in children: A focus on provision for Black children in the Early Years Foundation Stage'*. London: DCSF.

Pearce, S.S. (1996) *Flash of Insight: Metaphor and Narrative in Therapy*. Boston: Allyn and Bacon.

Pratt-Harris, N.C., Sinclair, M.M, Bragg, C.B., Williams, N.R., Ture, K.N., Smith, B.D., Marshall, Jr, I. and Brown, L. (2016) 'Police-involved Homicide of Unarmed Black Males: Observations by Black Scholars in the Midst of the April 2015 Baltimore Uprising'. *Journal of Human Behaviour in the Social Environment*, 26(3–4), pp. 377–389. Available at: https://www.tandfonline.com/doi/abs/10.1080/10911359 .2015.1132853.

Rosenthal, R. and Jacobson, L.F. (1968) 'Teacher Expectations for the Disadvantaged'. *Scientific American*, 218(4), pp. 19–23.

Ross, L. (1977) 'The Intuitive Psychologist and His Shortcomings: Distortions in the Attribution Process'. *Advances in Experimental Social Psychology*, 10, pp. 174–214.

Staples, B. (2014) 'At School, It Matters if You're Black or White'. *The New York Times*, 28 March. Available at: https://archive.nytimes.com/takingnote.blogs .nytimes.com/2014/03/28/at-school-it-matters-if-youre-black-or-white/.

Strand, S. (2012) 'The White British-Black Caribbean Achievement Gap: Tests, Tiers and Teacher Expectations'. *British Educational Research Journal*, 38(1), pp. 75–101.

Sylva, K., Melhuish, E., Sammons, P., Siraj-Blatchford, I., Taggart, B. (2004) *The Effective Provision of Pre-School Education (EPPE) Project: Final Report: A Longitudinal Study Funded by the DfES 1997–2004*. London: Sure Start. Available at: https://dera.ioe.ac.uk/8543/7/SSU-SF-2004-01.pdf.

Weir, K. (2016) 'Policing in Black and White'. *American Psychological Association*, 47(11), p. 36. Available at: https://www.apa.org/monitor/2016/12/cover-policing.

Yaafouri, L.E. (2018) 'Growing Through our Biases: An Educator Exercise'. *Diversifi-ed*, 8 January. Available at: https://diversifi-ed.com/explore/2018/9/22/growing -through-our-biases-an-educator-exercise.

3

The voice of the child

Hannah Betteridge, Stella Louis, and Liz Pemberton

When we critically examine our own, unconscious bias and understand the way racism is embedded within the constructs of our society, we become more aware of how our thought structures influence what we notice and how the things we notice are interpreted through the observation, assessment, and planning process. However, in our journey to become more self-aware, it is vital that we never lose sight of the fact that the children we care for must remain at the heart of what we do. Years of training have shown us that when we feel guilty, shameful, or embarrassed, it can be all too easy to overcorrect or overcompensate for mistakes that we have made in the past by focusing on the things we can control (e.g., adult-led activities) at the expense of other factors (e.g., how we respond to unexpected and challenging behaviours). No matter how well-intentioned, this one-sided approach will fail to have the desired impact if you are simultaneously unable to support and extend a child's self-initiated learning about race, diversity, and inclusion.

An essential part of the role of an educator is to provide a safe and supportive emotional environment for all children in all scenarios. This involves considering not only the impact of our attitudes and beliefs but our role in supporting, extending, and, at times, constructively challenging a child's independent learning in a developmentally appropriate way. To effectively support a child's personal, social, and emotional development, educators need to be able to flex and adapt their approach according to the unique needs of the individual child. This means providing them with space to express themselves and to voice their knowledge and understanding about race so that we may accurately assess where they are at and plan effectively to support their development.

A growing number of Western countries, including the UK, have championed a child-centred approach to early years provision that encourages educators to put the child at the centre of their practice in recognition of

DOI: 10.4324/9781003251149-4

the positive impact that this can have on a child's cognitive development. However, knowing how to strike the right balance between adult and child-led activities and discussions about race can be challenging. The answer is not straightforward: there is no one-size-fits-all approach when it comes to teaching children about race. The balance you strive for will ultimately depend on the needs of the children and the demographic makeup of the setting you are in. Only you and the team around you can do the work to identify what that balance should be, and we would encourage you to work with parents, carers, and the local community as you reflect on this. When educators engage in safe, candid, regular, and developmentally appropriate discussions about race and discrimination, the bias seen in children's behaviour and attitudes is lower (Katz, 2003).

As you think about how you can develop and embed an anti-bias and anti-racist approach within your practice, it is imperative that you consider the voice of the child, as well as your own attitudes and beliefs. This is the only way to ensure that you are providing holistic and truly meaningful support to the children in your setting.

Reflective questions

- How have you built the voice of the child into your pedagogical practice?
- How do you encourage and support children to be themselves?
- How do you ensure that each child is valued?
- How do you know that you are meeting each child's needs in your setting?

Responding to race

The myth that children don't see race is severely damaging. Not only can it prevent parents, carers, and educators from giving children the tools they need to navigate the world around them, but it can also lead to schools dismissing and failing to address racist incidents. How we respond to these incidents matters on both a micro individual level and a macro structural level. Shrugging off problematic behaviour because a child is 'too young' or 'it was just a joke' diminishes the very real effect that such actions can have on another child's self-identity and sense of self-worth. It also teaches the child perpetrating the behaviour that their actions are acceptable.

As we discuss elsewhere in this book, studies suggest that from the age of two, children not only categorise others by race, but they begin to internalise racial biases that they come across from their interactions with parents, families, picture books, movies, and television (Hirschfeld, 2008; Louis, 2023). Just like us, children ingest racism from the world around them. It is a fallacy to think that they are immune to its effects. You can see it in a child's use of phrases like 'us' and 'them', in who they choose to engage with and how they engage with them, and in how they describe colour.

Within academia, knowledge about how beliefs and stereotypes about gender affect a child's sense of identity and behaviour has been well studied. For example, Associate Professor in Early Childhood and Director of the Centre for Equity and Inclusion in Early Childhood, Glenda MacNaughton argues that children's pretend play reveals a rich tapestry of information about what they believe women and men are capable of and the roles they should assume with society. This is evident when they play at 'having babies' or 'making a hospital' (MacNaughton, 1999: 81). Indeed, 'storylines structure young children's dramatic play and offer us one way to see how they are making sense of gender in their lives and the lives of other children' (MacNaughton, 2000: 81). The same principle applies to children's understanding of race relations. Through observing the storylines that children explore in their play, the power balance of the characters they inhabit and the language they use, we can gather a wealth of information about their attitudes about themselves and others. How we, as educators, respond to these clues offers a key means to either address, perpetuate, or challenge existing societal inequalities.

Case study – *Dadaji*

Amandeep is a three-year-old boy who has attended his nursery since he was six months old. The setting is located in Harborne in Birmingham, England. He is Indian and Sikh and was born in Birmingham, England, which is home to a diverse population. He has always lived with his family; his parents Sonia and Baldeep were born in Britain and his older sister Kiran is seven. Amandeep wears a *patka* (a small hair covering sometimes worn by Sikh boys) and is an assertive and happy child. He often tells Sharon, his key worker who is Black British with Caribbean heritage, that his *Dadaji* (Grandad) is very funny when he is at the *Gurdwara* (a place of worship for Sikhs). Amandeep says that he does 'lots of loud singing' and that 'mummy was dancing with her Sari on'.

Sharon grew up in Birmingham, England in the 1980s and knows of the history of many South Asian, Sikh communities who settled in that part of the city, having migrated from India. Her own grandparents arrived in Birmingham from Jamaica in the 1950s and settled in Handsworth where they still live now.

Sharon tells Amandeep that she would love for him to teach her some of the songs that *Dadaji* sings at the *Gurdwara*. Sharon is careful to mirror the language that Amandeep uses and does not replace it with the English translation. Amandeep tells her, 'You have to learn Punjabi first! Can you talk Punjabi? My Daddy says you have to be Indian!' Sharon responds, 'Ok, that's fine. I'm not Indian but I think that you can still teach me. I'd like to learn'. She follows him to the carpet area where she sits on a beanbag cross-legged and says, 'Let's go! Teach me! I'm ready!' Amandeep laughs and sits on her lap whilst singing a song in Punjabi.

Amandeep tells Sharon that he loves to sing loudly, and Sharon says that she does too. She claps whilst he sings, and he claps too on beat with his song. The other children see what is happening and come over to where Sharon and Amandeep are. They jump up and down and start singing.

One of the children, Aaron, exclaims, 'Amandeep, you're not talking English. That sounds like muggly maggly' in a disparaging tone and laughs. The other children laugh too. Amandeep immediately stops singing and looks upset.

Sharon tells everybody to quieten down and explains to the child who made the remark that calling Amandeep's words 'muggly maggly' was unkind. She reiterates that Amandeep was singing a beautiful song from the *Gurdwara*. She says, 'We should all use our listening ears like I was, to learn the song that Amandeep is teaching us'. Sharon gently encourages Amandeep to carry on and urges the other children to carry on dancing if they want to but to listen to the song whilst Amandeep is singing.

Amandeep carries on but stays seated on Sharon's lap.

Take a moment to consider the following questions. You might find it helpful to write down your thoughts and revisit these questions at the end of the book.

- How does Amandeep demonstrate a strong sense of his own cultural, racial, and/or religious identity in this interaction?
- Thinking about her words and her behaviour, how does Sharon support and extend Amandeep's sense of self-identity? What impact is this likely to have on Amandeep?
- How does Sharon validate Amandeep's experience?
- Was Sharon right to address the impact of Aaron's words publicly in front of the other children?
- How does Sharon ensure that the other children engage respectfully?
- How might Sharon's own lived experience have equipped her to engage with Amandeep? Without this experience, how can someone prepare themselves to deal with these situations appropriately?
- Is a follow-up conversation necessary with Amandeep or his parents? If you answered no, why? If you answered yes, how would you handle this discussion?
- Is a follow-up discussion necessary with Aaron or his parents/carers? If you answered no, why? If you answered yes, how would you handle this discussion?
- If this happened in your setting, what follow-up activities could you plan to provide space for the children in your care to learn more about the beauty and strength that can be found in diversity and inclusion?

Throughout this example, Sharon carefully positions herself as the learner and Amandeep as the teacher to support Amandeep's exploration of his culture and extend this learning opportunity. She asks pertinent questions about the songs he could teach her and provides a secure base both emotionally and physically so that this can take place. This shows Amandeep that it is safe to be himself, and that his cultural and religious identity is valued by those around him. Her approach throughout is empowering and reaffirming, giving Amandeep the space to use his voice.

However, this situation could easily have gone differently, and it is important to consider the impact that a different approach may have had on both Amandeep and the other children in the setting. Sharon could have dismissed or minimised Amandeep's description of his family at the *Gurdwara* by suggesting that they have the conversation at another time, rather than recognising the opportunity for a teachable moment. She could have suggested that they save the teaching of the song for their Diwali celebrations, thus tokenising this moment. In response to Aaron's behaviour, Sharon could have chosen not to address the derogatory comment he made or laughed it off as a joke. She could have prioritised her own knowledge about Amandeep's faith and corrected him based on her own lived experience of having grown up with Sikh communities. What impact do you think these actions would have had?

In all the alternative scenarios we set out above, it is likely that Sharon's actions would have diminished Amandeep's enthusiasm and taught him a subtle lesson about the value placed on who he is by society by marginalising and sidelining his beliefs. A complex understanding of all the factors at play here is required and it is in this depth and breadth of understanding that we can become the best version of ourselves as practitioners and start to truly value all the gifts that our children have to give.

Seeing colour

To support children in developing a positive self-identity where they feel happy and confident in who they are, we also need to consider how we can effectively counter negative attitudes that they may have internalised about themselves and others on the basis of their race. We cannot control the messages that the children in our settings absorb from the outside world, but we can give them the tools to question their assumptions and beliefs to help them better understand and love who they are.

 ## Case study – pretty in pink

Soraya is two and a half years old. She is a shy child who attends nursery in Quedgeley, Gloucester, a predominantly White British town in England. Her mum, Sam, is White British, and her dad, Isaac, is Black British with Nigerian heritage. Soraya grew up in Quedgeley and lives with her mum. She doesn't see her dad or his side of the family much as he has a high-pressured job abroad and his parents have retired in Nigeria. Soraya is the only child at her nursery who is not White and she often tells her key worker Oscar, who is White, that she misses her mummy.

One day, Oscar decides to set up a painting station for creative drawing, laying out a selection of different coloured paints. Soraya wonders over to the painting station and begins to draw a picture of her and her mum, using the pink paint to draw both her and her mother's faces, even though she is mixed-race, and her face is brown.

Oscar does not interrupt Soraya's painting activity, tells her that it is a beautiful painting, and displays it in the room.

When Sam comes to collect Soraya, Oscar shows her the painting and Sam expresses concern. She tells Oscar that he should not have let Soraya choose the pink paint. Oscar gets upset and says that he does not see Soraya's colour and that it is not important because it is how Soraya sees herself.

- Why do you think Soraya's mother, Sam, showed concern?
- What might Soraya's choice to use the pink paint tell you about (a) how she sees herself; and (b) how she has internalised the representations of people who have her skin colour?
- Did Oscar support Soraya's sense of self-identity in the activity? How, or how not?
- How might Oscar's description of the painting as 'beautiful' have reaffirmed Soraya's internalised beliefs about race?
- Is there anything else that Oscar could have done to support Soraya to develop a positive sense of her racial identity during this activity?
- Outside of this activity, how else could Oscar have ensured that Soraya (a) felt represented in the setting; and (b) had the tools to discuss her race?

Educators are essential pieces of the jigsaw puzzle that help to shape children's identities in every sense, including how they feel about the colour of their skin and how they feel about the race and ethnicity of others. When we consider Oscar's response, it is clear his colour-blind approach meant he missed an opportunity to have an important discussion about how Soraya feels about her own skin colour.

As educators, it is important that we provide space for children to voice their truth and explore their motivations to unpick where they are in their personal, social, and emotional development journey. By ignoring the issue, we can unwittingly reinforce the beliefs a child may have internalised about Whiteness being 'good' and 'desirable' and Blackness being a 'bad' or 'undesirable' characteristic. Gently probing Soraya with open and neutral questions could have been a helpful way to give her space to articulate her belief system, including what qualities she thinks the world values and what qualities the world does not. The insight that an educator can obtain from discussion like this can provide a powerful foundation for them to sensitively provide a meaningful counter-narrative that supports children to develop a more positive sense of self without judgement.

The use of resources, such as the book *Our Skin* by Megan Madison and Jessica Ralli (2021) or *My Skin, Your Skin* by Laura Henry-Allain (2021), can also provide a helpful scaffold for conversations about the range of colours skin comes in, and why each colour is special and beautiful. Embedding these resources into educational settings can help children experiencing similar identity challenges as Soraya to feel affirmed about the colour of their skin. They can also support educators to find the appropriate language to use when talking about race with a child. It is just as important that we make space for these discussions and provide inclusive resources in White-majority areas, where children of colour may struggle to see themselves represented in the world around them and White children may grow up without any direct experience of people of a different racial or ethnic background to themselves, as it is in racially diverse geographical regions.

Exercise

How can you use a child's knowledge of their culture to support their learning and development within the curriculum?

Draw up an action plan, showing how you and everyone involved in working with the child plan to support their understanding. You might find it helpful to use the following headings: cultural origin, religion, language, and play experiences. Plan opportunities to involve parents and/or carers to discuss the important cultural events or traditions in their lives. Give your colleagues an opportunity to discuss their own understanding, attitudes, and opinions about the child. Consider how you will bring your ideas together and what milestones you want to set, building in opportunities for reflection.

Race, identity, and belonging

It can be easy to dismiss the examples we have provided in this chapter as one-offs and downplay the impact that these singular events can have on a child, or how much they can tell us about children's self-identity and beliefs about race. In her memoir, *More Than Enough*, Elaine Welteroth, a mixed-race American journalist and former editor of *Teen Vogue*, provides a forceful account of just how significant and formative a child's experience can be. Whilst in preschool, her teacher asked the class to make a collage that represented their family using magazines. Elaine describes the first time she understood that race was an issue:

> I saw smiling White ladies in pristine kitchens, cute White babies wearing Pull-Ups, handsome White men in tailored suits, White kids picnicking on Crayola-green grass. I had never heard anyone use terms like 'representation' before; all I knew was no one on any of those magazine pages looked like me or my family. It reinforced what I had somehow already internalized: I was different […]

> At that age, when a teacher hands you a pair of scissors, a glue stick, and a stack of magazines filled with White people, and asks you to cut out pictures that look like your family, you do what anyone living in a hyper-White world would do – and what all of my classmates were doing – you cut out White people […]

> The [Teaching Assistant] TA slyly pulled out the sole Black magazine I hadn't touched [… and] flipped to another Black girl who looked nothing like me. 'Oh, what about her? She reminds me so much of you. Her hair is just like yours.' She laughed awkwardly. I froze, ashamed.

> I got the message: I was supposed to be cutting out brown people […] but adding a Black mom, a Black brother, a Black me to this White paper family I was constructing would have meant having to own that I was not like the rest of my classmates […]

> Only as an adult in quiet moments of reflection can I begin to see clearly the subconscious impact of White supremacy at work in the messages I was fed as a child. By centring and position Whiteness as superior, Whiteness as the norm, and everything else as a deviation, a racial hierarchy is reinforced […] I grew up with an unspoken suspicion that the world would see me as second best, too.

(Welteroth, 2019: 15–20)

As children start to make sense of who they are in a racialised society, it is important that we know how to recognise and counter any indicators of children showing signs of internalised racism. In educational settings, we can see this play out in a multitude of ways, from a Black child declaring their preference for a White doll and attributing positive traits to a White doll and not a Black one (Clark and Clark, 1947) or, as in the case of Soraya and Elaine, a child choosing to depict themselves as a race different to their own.

> **Internalised racism** is defined by sociologist Karen D. Pyke (2010) as 'the internalisation of racial oppression by the racially subordinated'.

Former educator and politician, Bernard Coard, explains that signs of internalised racism can also be seen in how children choose to portray others (2021). Bernard Coard is Black and spent two years teaching in England before publishing a book on the pervasive bias he had witnessed in the British educational system against Black children in 1971. In his book, Coard describes an incident where a White student drew a picture of him which included several key identifying traits: his glasses, his moustache, and his beard. However, the student did not colour in Coard's skin. When Coard asked the child why he had forgotten to do this, the child replied, 'I can't do that!' and walked to the other side of the room. The child, having admired Coard as his favourite teacher, could not accept that Coard was Black. He could not reconcile the positive qualities that he saw in his teacher with the messages that he had absorbed from the world around him about what it meant to be Black; messages which had created 'the most fearful image of what Black people were supposed to be like' (Coard, 2021: 27–28).

When we understand the way in which society operates within a racialised framework and hierarchy, and we acknowledge that this hierarchy is upheld structurally and systemically in our everyday lives, it is not surprising to see how even children internalise this messaging too. Whether we are racialised as White, Black, or Brown, it is important for us to all understand the constructs of a racialised society so that we can understand why the simple act of choosing pink paint rather than brown can be so damaging if left unchallenged.

The power of action

The messages that children ingest about racial difference can ultimately lead to covert or overt forms of racism. Both are serious and can have devastating effects on the children in our settings. The Macpherson Report, which looked into the investigation of Stephen Lawrence's brutal murder, defined a racist incident 'as any incident that is perceived to be racist by the victim or any other person' (1999). This includes derogatory name calling, threats, insults, exclusion from activities or conversations, physical violence, or encouraging another person to engage in any of the activities listed above on the basis of someone's race. All educational settings should have well-defined policies and procedures that set out how to respond to such incidents, and these should be clearly understood by the staff, children, and their families.

Case study – the ice-cream gang

In a small school in Somerset, a group of six five-year-old White girls was pretending to play a game about being in a gang during lunchtime. Somerset is a large rural county in South West England, with a majority White population.

Two five-year-old Black girls, Stacey and Rachael, who were both from the same reception class as the girls in the gang, asked if they could join the game. Rebecca, adopting the role of gang leader, replied briskly, 'No!'. When Rachael asked why, Rebecca said: 'We're the vanilla ice-cream gang. You can't be in our gang 'cos you're chocolate'. Stacey and Rachael walked away; they were confused, angry, hurt, and sad. As they headed inside, Stacey started to cry.

Ria, their reception class teacher, was in the main building overseeing another activity. When she saw Stacey crying, she asked what was wrong. Rachael explained what had happened: 'Miss, Rebecca wouldn't let us play with her because she said we're chocolate'. Not knowing how to address the situation, Ria said, 'Don't worry about it, girls. Why don't you go and play your own game?'

Stacey and Rachael looked at Ria in silence, with tears now falling down both of their faces. They walked away together, finding a quiet corner and disengaged from the rest of the day's activities.

In a group training session on race a few months later, Ria reflected on this interaction, recounting how she felt uncomfortable and out of her depth when confronted with this situation. She told the group that she did not know how to support Stacey and Rachael, or how to constructively challenge the young girls in the gang in a way that would encourage greater empathy and acceptance of difference. Not wanting to make it worse by getting it wrong, in that moment, she felt like doing nothing was the safest choice.

- What does Rebecca's language and behaviour tell you about her understanding of race?
- What impact did Ria's actions and inaction have on (a) Stacey and Rachael and (b) Rebecca and the rest of the gang?
- How could Ria have handled the situation differently?
- Are follow-up discussions required with either Stacey and Rachael or their families, or Rebecca or her family? What about the other five young girls in the gang who didn't say anything?
- Does your setting have processes in place to deal with racist incidents and counter discriminatory words or behaviours? How do these processes support a child who is a victim of this event, and how do they support the perpetrator?

Ria is not alone. Whether we buy into the myth that children are colour-blind or not, talking about race is still a social taboo in Western societies because it requires us to accept things that many would rather remain hidden. A 2020 UK study into race at work found that only four in ten people are comfortable discussing race in the workplace (Business in the Community, 2021). This discomfort is why we begin many of our training sessions with a simple exercise: we ask attendees to put their hands up if they have ever felt uncomfortable talking about race. Often, the vast majority of people on the course raise their hands. This can be due to a multitude of reasons, including a fear of getting it wrong (e.g., using the wrong language), feelings of awkwardness, or a misguided concern that discussing race makes you racist. What may surprise you is that when we ask this question, we also raise our hands. Although we may be anti-racist educators and activists, we would be lying if we said talking about race is natural and comfortable for us either. We have the same fear that we could get things wrong; after all, language changes and time moves on. At times, discussing race can feel heavy, draining, and triggering. You never know what someone is going to say in response to the points you make, and this uncertainty can breed fear and trepidation. However, over time what we have learnt is that silence strangles progress. So, we embrace the discomfort. We push through it. We make space to understand why it makes us feel so uncomfortable and do something about it.

Reflective questions

Ask yourself:

- When it comes to discussing race and racism with the children in your setting, how comfortable do you feel? What could you do better? What would make you more comfortable?
- Now ask yourself the same questions about discussing race and racism with (a) their parents and/or carers; and (b) your colleagues.

Racial trauma

In 2021, the mental health charity Mind found that 55% of young people from Black and Black British backgrounds had experienced racism at school. For young people from mixed-race backgrounds, the number was 57%, and for those from Asian or Asian British backgrounds, the study found just over a third (36%) had experienced it too. Of all those that said they had experienced racism at school, 70% said that it had negatively impacted their mental health (Mind, 2021). In the same year, the British newspaper *The Guardian* found that UK schools had recorded more than 60,000 racist incidents over a five-year period, with the true figure believed to be considerably higher as many incidents either are not reported or not recorded (Batty and Parveen, 2021). Just one year prior, when conducting a similar exercise, the BBC found that primary-school exclusions for racism had risen by 40% in just over a decade (McCamley, 2020).

Admittedly this data could be said to go beyond the realm of this book, as it focuses on the experiences of children and young people throughout their educational journey, not just on their time in early years settings. However, these indicators are all we have. Following the UK Government's decision to remove the legal requirement for educational settings to report racist incidents to local authorities in 2012, it has become incredibly challenging to obtain a true picture of how these statistics play out for under-fives in Britain. In light of the pervasive nature of the problem and the fact that children start to see race from as young as six months, it would be logical to assume under-fives are unlikely to be exempt from waves of racism or the mental anguish demonstrated in the studies above. Indeed, as Professor David Gillborn highlights: 'If the evidence that we can get points to there being an epidemic of racism in schools and yet there is no reliable data at a national level, then the government can't guarantee that they're meeting basic safeguarding [needs]' (quoted in Batty and Parveen, 2021). On a micro level, we believe that the same is true for individual settings. If you do not have processes and structures in place to report and record incidents in your setting, how can you adequately safeguard children and claim to meet their personal, social, and emotional development needs?

Radical psychologist, Guilaine Kinouani, notes that Black children in particular are usually invisible from discussions about the immediate and lifelong impact of racism, despite its horrific effects (2021). And yet, the series of adverse childhood experiences that children endure because of their race, like being told that your language is 'muggly maggly' or that you cannot play with your friends because of the colour of your skin, 'creates a context of chronic stress that can cumulatively have a traumatic effect', with 'lifelong negative emotional and physical' consequences (Kinouani, 2021). We cannot afford to be blind to our role in this. If we remain silent when we see racist incidents play out, we leave a void that will often be filled by anxiety and self-loathing. We teach children that their feelings are not valued and being subjected to discriminatory and prejudicial treatment is normal. What does that do to their self-esteem? How does it impact their cognitive development?

We have a pedagogical responsibility to ensure that all the children in our settings leave our care with a positive sense of identity, and that includes their racial identity. If they observe that we are reluctant to challenge racism when we see it, we cannot credibly build an environment where they feel safe exploring their social, cultural, and racial identity with us, or where they feel comfortable asking us questions or feel equipped to come to us when they experience racism. Instead, we stunt their growth. We place the burden on them, having already been oppressed, to process their pain or confusion alone.

Developing a secure emotional environment

In each of the case studies we explored in this chapter – *Dadaji*, *Pretty in Pink*, and *the Ice-Cream Gang* – we asked a variation of the following question:

would you have a follow-up conversation with the children named in the examples? To set these conversations up for success, we need to create a safe and supportive emotional environment in which young children are supported to express themselves and know that it is okay to be vulnerable. After all, 'only when a child feels emotionally safe and secure in their environment will they undertake the challenge and risk needed to learn' (Bruce, 2010). But how do we do this?

As a first step, it is vital that educators recognise and understand that all children are unique and deserve to be treated as such. They will have their own personality, likes, dislikes, strengths, and weaknesses. Children need to be given the time and space to explore their identity in an environment that is free from bias, where they are valued for who they are and their unique contribution, and where they see others of a different racial background to themselves being valued and respected for who they are, too. To do this, we must strive to be fair and consistent in how we observe, support, and manage children's behaviour. Critically examining our own personal bias is an important precursor to this (see Chapter 2).

As educators, we also need to have an awareness and understanding of children's backgrounds and cultural identities to find ways to meaningfully embed their language, cultural practices, and positive examples of representation into our everyday provision, without tokenising their experience (Louis and Betteridge, 2020). Our observations provide a powerful tool for doing this. For example, one day key worker Serena was singing the nursery rhyme *Five Little Ducks* with a group of three-year-olds in her setting. She noticed that Anni, a young Syrian girl, was replacing the word 'duck' with the word 'batta'. Over the next few days, Serena monitored Anni, sharing her findings with Anni's mother. Anni's mother mentioned that Anni liked to play with farm animals at home, so Serena did some research and learnt how to say a few different farm animals in Arabic. The next time Serena observed Anni playing with farm animals, Serena went and sat with her. Serena said the word horse in Arabic. Anni looked surprised and smiled before erupting into giggles. By taking time to learn Anni's mother tongue and placing emphasis on Anni's voice, Serena sent Anni a powerful message about the value and importance of her experience and understanding of the world. Acknowledging the diverse experiences that children have is vital if we are to create a secure emotional environment in which children feel safe and free to express themselves and their feelings, no matter how challenging they might be.

Beyond their use of language, we see children express themselves in a range of ways, including through their behaviour, clothes, hairstyles, and emotions. As educators, we need to learn how to respond respectfully and appropriately regardless of the method of expression a child chooses, and we need to do so with a meaningful understanding of the social, cultural, and emotional environment that the child is operating in. Take emotion: a child may choose to dance when excited or show their mood through their facial expressions. They may avoid making eye contact with adults in the setting when they are being spoken to, or they may become noticeably quiet during adult-led activities, particularly in comparison to the way in which they engage or play with their friends, as a result of the cultural norms they have been exposed to at home. Our role is to support children to express and manage their emotions in a developmentally appropriate way, without judgement. They need to know that they are respected, accepted, and supported by us. To do this, we must strive to build strong relationships with the children in our settings that enable us to understand their individual ways of communicating, including how they express emotional cues. We can acknowledge and validate their feelings, letting them know that we see and hear them for who they are.

However, when we combine our observations of a child's self-expression with assumptions about their motives, our unconscious bias can bleed into our assessments, making us more likely to misunderstand the way in which children behave and choose to express themselves. This can lead to children being inaccurately labelled as disengaged and disrespectful, having challenging behaviour, or having additional learning needs. The result is an emotional environment that is unable to support the child and educators who are unable to hear and respond to the voice of the child. Striving to keep an open mind, with an awareness of our own bias and a willingness to meet a child at the stage that they are at, is key to preventing this.

Giving children meaningful feedback when they show us how they see and understand their own culture is another important tool to demonstrate that we see and value who they are. Saying 'ok' or 'well done' is not enough if we want children to feel a sense of pride and confidence in their culture. We should be specific and authentic in our praise; for example,

> I like the way you explained to Jack why you call me and the other teachers 'auntie' It is so kind of you to share your culture with him and explain the different ways of showing respect to the grownups you meet at home and in the community.

This form of praise not only shows that we value the child's culture, but actively welcomes and encourages them to share it with others.

We need to create a secure space for children to learn, explore, and test ideas without fear. Internationally renowned German educator Friedrich Froebel notes that

> we find a freshness in the life of the child who has been rightly guided and cared for in his early years. Is there any part of a person's thought and feelings, knowledge, and ability, which does not have its deepest root in childhood, and any aspect of his future education which does not originate there?

He highlights the long-term impact of environments that cater to the needs of the unique child (as quoted in Lilley, 1967: 87).

Children also need to have the language, both verbal and non-verbal, to express themselves and regulate their emotions. By letting children know that you understand what they are going through, you can help them to name, label, and acknowledge their own emotions. This is particularly important where a child may be experiencing racial trauma as a result of their experiences in or outside of the setting. Working with them to deal with the cause of their anxiety and acknowledging their worries is hugely important to enable children to externalise their concerns so that they can be properly addressed. Children rely on us to help them develop the knowledge and skills to be resilient. As a result, we have a pedagogical responsibility to strengthen children's abilities to recognise, manage, and control their emotions to support them as they grow into adults and set them up for success. As Goleman argues,

> [i]f your emotional abilities aren't in hand, if you don't have self-awareness, if you are not able to manage distressing emotions, if you can't have empathy and have effective relationships, then no matter how smart you are, you are not going to get very far.
>
> (1998: 275)

Children are not born with self-esteem; instead, this is something that develops through their interactions with people, materials, and the environment as they grow. As educators, we play a critical role in providing children with positive learning opportunities that engage and motivate them, boosting their self-esteem and confidence. Supporting each child to develop a positive self-image is an important part of educators' work. This includes helping young children to understand how they are alike in some ways and how they can be different in others. We should encourage children to talk positively about their physical characteristics and those of others around them. This should be supplemented by positive depictions of diversity and inclusion embedded within their physical environment to counter damaging stereotypes and promote equality (see Chapter 4 for more information and guidance on how to do this). Educators can source a range of developmentally appropriate resources and educational materials to provide children with opportunities where they can look at and explore materials that challenge prejudice alongside a knowledgeable educator.

Derman-Sparks and the ABC Taskforce (1989) encourage educators to guide and expand children's understanding of race by sharing books and other authentic visual images, as this can show children that someone's race cannot constrain what they can achieve. For example, showing images and newspaper clippings that depict Black men and women engaged in a range of different professions, including scientists, doctors, actresses, politicians, soldiers, or the police, can encourage children to ask questions, whilst making the invisible more authentically visible. Educators can also create meaningful scenarios in which children develop their empathic skills in response to others – asking children how would they feel or what would they do if…? This naturally creates teachable moments to facilitate discussions with children about respect, diversity, and difference.

Teaching children to value diversity and difference is an ongoing part of the educators' role. Regardless of whether children experience or witness racism directly, they need to feel that they can come to us with their concerns and they will be taken seriously, without bias or judgement. Children also need to be equipped to address situations as and when they arise. As Lane (2008: 233) notes:

> Children should be encouraged to learn that they, too, have a role to play in taking responsibility to tell adults when they witness any form of unkindness, racial abuse or name-calling. Young children can be encouraged to recognise it happening to themselves and others and to tell an adult, without going through the feeling of believing that they have betrayed a member of the group. If they can be helped to see that both the wronged person and the perpetrator will be supported, they may be willing more willing to come forward.

71

Establishing and developing a genuine relationship with parents and carers can also be an important way to create emotional safety for the children in our care. These relationships enable us to gather useful information about the child's needs, relationships, and preferences. Working together with a child's parents or carers, we can therefore identify meaningful ways to support their child's learning, including listening to any worries or concerns that they may have. This partnership requires educators to be open to learn from and with parents' knowledge of the child and cultural practices. It also requires educators to provide regular information to parents about how children learn.

Reflective questions

As you continue to reflect on your practice, consider the following:

- How are you providing opportunities for children to develop a sense of identity?
- Do you know how each child's family teaches them about their own culture?
- How do you show that you accept and value each child's contribution?
- How do you support and guide children to know their capabilities and who they are?
- How do you support and guide children to know that they are part of a family?
- How do you support and guide children to know that they are special to someone?
- How do you support and guide children to feel at home in the school or setting?
- How do you support and guide children to feel part of a group?
- How do you support and guide children to show respect for others?
- How do you support and guide children to develop their self-identity and attitudes towards others?

The change that we want to see in society must be nurtured from an early age. The challenge, if we are up to it, is to set the foundations for future generations to actively challenge racism and think more critically about what our individual roles are in doing this as early years educators, parents, and carers who should see ourselves as people actively committed to social justice and equity.

References

Batty, D. and Parveen, N. (2021) 'UK Schools Record More Than 60,000 Racist Incidents in Five Years'. *The Guardian*, 28 March. Available at: https://www.theguardian.com/education/2021/mar/28/uk-schools-record-more-than-60000-racist-incidents-five-years.

Bruce, C. (2010) *Emotional Literacy in the Early Years*. London: SAGE.

Business in the Community (2021) *Race at Work 202 Scorecard Report: McGregor-Smith Review Four Years On*. Available at: https://www.bitc.org.uk/wp-content/uploads/2021/10/bitc-race-report-raceatwork2021scorecardreport-oct2021.pdf.

Clark, K.B. and Clark, M.P. (1947) 'Racial Identification and Preference in Negro Children'. In T.M. Newcomb and E.L. Hartley (eds.) *Readings in Social Psychology*. New York: Rinehart & Winston, pp. 602–611.

Coard, B. (2021) *How the West Indian Child is Made Educationally Sub-Normal in the British School System*. Expanded 5th edn. Kingston: McDermott Publishing.

Derman-Sparks, L. and the ABC Taskforce (1989) *Anti-bias Curriculum: Tools for Empowering Young Children*. Washington DC: National Association for the Education of Young Children.

Goleman, D. (1998) *Working with Emotional Intelligence*. London: Bloomsbury.

Henry-Allain, L. (2021) *My Skin, Your Skin: An Early Introduction to Race and Racism*. London: Penguin.

Hirschfeld, L.A. (2008) 'Children's Developing Conceptions of Race'. In S.M. Quintana and C. McKown (eds.) *Handbook of Race, Racism, and the Developing Child*. New Jersey: John Wiley & Sons, Inc., pp. 37–54.

Jane, L. (2008) *Young Children and Racial Justice: Taking Action for Racial Equality*. London: National Children's Bureau.

Katz, P.A. (2003) 'Racists or Tolerant Multiculturalists? How Do They Begin?' *American Psychologist*, 58(11), pp. 897–909.

Kinouani, G. (2021) *Living While Black: The Essential Guide to Overcoming Racial Trauma*. London: Ebury Press.

Lilley, I. (1967) *Friedrich Froebel: A Selection from His Writing*. Cambridge: Cambridge University Press.

Louis, S. (2023) 'Race, Anti-Discrimination and Work to Combat the Effects of Discrimination on Practitioners and Children'. In S. Cave and N. Meah (eds.) *Early Education: Current Realities and Future Priorities*. London: Sage, pp. 95–106.

Louis, S. and Betteridge, H. (2020) 'Let's Talk About Bias in the Early Years'. *Famly*, 16 September. Available at: https://www.famly.co/blog/bias-in-early-years.

MacNaughton, G. (1999) 'Even Pink Tents Have Glass Ceilings: Crossing the Gender Boundaries in Pretend Play'. In E. Dau (ed.) *Child's Play: Revisiting play in Early Childhood Settings'.* SydneyMacLennan and Petty Pty Ltd. pp. 81–96.

MacNaughton, G. (2000) *Rethinking Gender in Early Childhood Education.* London: SAGE.

Macpherson, W. (1999) *The Stephen Lawrence Inquiry: Report of an Inquiry by Sir William MacPherson of Cluny.* London: The Stationary Office.

McCamley, F. (2020) 'Exclusions for Racism in Primary Schools in England up more than 40%'. *BBC News,* 1 January. Available at: https://www.bbc.co.uk/news/education-50331687.

Madison, M. and Ralli, J. (2021) *Our Skin: A First Conversation About Race.* London: Penguin.

Mind (2021) *Not Making the Grade: Why Our Approach to Mental Health at Secondary School is Failing Young People.* Available at: https://www.mind.org.uk/media/8860/not-making-the-grade-summary.pdf.

Pyke, K.D. (2010) 'What Is Internalized Racial Oppression and Why Don't We Study it? Acknowledging Racism's Hidden Injuries'. *Sociological Perspectives,* 53(4), pp. 551–572.

Welteroth, E. (2019) *More Than Enough: Claiming Space for Who You Are (No Matter What They Say).* London: Ebury Press.

Part 2
Transforming the learning environment

4

Race and representation in the early years

Stella Louis and Hannah Betteridge

If you can see it, you can be it – or so the saying goes. At an early age, children develop strong ideas about what they 'can' or 'can't' do and be. The representations that they see are therefore hugely important; not only can they give children a window into a world of possibilities, but they have the power to reinforce or dismantle prejudice that children may have unwittingly absorbed elsewhere.

Providing authentic and meaningful representations within educational settings can help support children to better understand the world that they live in. They can teach children to respect and embrace difference in all its splendour and enable children of all races to feel valued and included. When young children do not see people like themselves represented in the books they read, the items they play with or the music they are surrounded by, it can profoundly affect their sense of belonging (Derman-Sparks and Edwards, 2019). Children need to be able to see themselves and cultural practices represented in the learning environment to thrive. The 'invisibility or visibility' of diverse and authentic representation in an educational setting, whether conscious or not, can ultimately prevent Black and Brown children from developing a positive sense of self, while strengthening and normalising the primacy of Whiteness for White children (Derman-Sparks and Edwards, 2019).

The importance of creating a positive sense of self

From birth, children begin to learn what it means to be themselves. Through their exploration of the world around them, they figure out who they are, what they like, and what they don't like. As educators, we have a responsibility to support children to develop a positive sense of self and create a sense of belonging for the children within our settings. The beliefs they develop during their childhood about what they can do and what they can become form an intractable foundation for their personal, social, and emotional development, guiding their adolescent and adult lives. Its importance cannot be overstated: that is why the United Nations (UN) *Convention on the Rights of the Child* enshrined a child's legal right to educational provision that supports the development of their personality, talents, and abilities, alongside the development of respect for their own culture and cultures different to their own (UN, 1989).

To effectively support a child to feel confident, loved, and valued, we also need to be aware of how a child's self-identity is constructed. This knowledge will help to ensure that children are exposed to representations of people just like them in an authentic and meaningful way.

Children are part of a family – they develop within the context of the relationships around them – and it is within this familial environment that children gain a sense of who they are (Louis, 2022). For many children, their transition to early years education will be the first time they experience different values and norms from the ones they are used to seeing at home. Through the structure and environment of the settings they are in, 'they may discover that certain ways of being (symbolised through appearance, clothes, possessions, activities, etc.) are favoured over others, that certain language groups are more valued than others, [or] that certain family compositions are more 'normal' than others' (Vandenbroeck, 2008: 26). During this time, they may be expected to conform to different cultural expectations or find that their cultural identity is rejected when those around them have difficulty with and quickly dismiss the correct pronunciation of their name. All these factors influence the way in which each child develops their sense of self-identity and self-worth.

There is a risk that through their exposure to these different ideas and values, children learn to see themselves as either 'the other' or 'the norm', with value judgements placed on one being 'right' and the other being 'wrong'. Both are inherently problematic. Our job is to be aware of the complex web of influence that can affect the development of a child's identity and support them as they navigate their way through the world until they learn, as Maya Angelou so beautifully put it, 'that in diversity there is beauty and there is strength'.

Noticing skin colour

You may have been told that 'children don't see race', but this is a myth. Research shows that at just six months old, a child can recognise differences in skin colour (Kelly *et al.*, 2005). By the age of two and a half, children show a preference for people like them, preferring to play with other children who are similar in race and gender (Katz and Kofkin, 1997; Hirschfeld, 2008). By three years old, children form judgements about people based on their race, and they begin to demonstrate signs of unconscious bias against other ethnicities (Derman-Sparks and Edwards, 2019). (More information on the studies exploring how children see race can be found in Chapter 1.)

The good news is that these views and judgements are not fixed: they are simply born out of our instinct for familiarity. With the right support, children can find the language to describe who they are and the world around them, without one race or ethnicity being centred as the 'norm' whilst others are framed as less than. No matter how uncomfortable we are talking about race, silence is never the answer. If we say nothing, children will learn to fill the void with their own stories. 'If they hear nothing about race, they figure out that there's something different about that topic. And that difference can become imbued with negativity' (Dr Wanjiku Njoroge as quoted in Belli, 2020).

Whether we like it or not, children notice similarities and differences in skin colour, hair styles, eye colour, and clothing. They may ask questions, such as, 'Why is he/she Black?' Or 'Why am I called Black, when my skin is brown?' They may want to talk about changes in skin colour, such as going brown or red when exposed to sunshine, or they may make reference to their skin tone in relation to other things: 'My mummy said I have caramel skin'.

These topics and questions should not be ignored – they are teachable moments to talk to children about their own identity and the differences that they observe. As an educator, you have a key role to play in helping children by providing them with factual information, rather than tokenistic or sweeping generalisations, so that they can take pride in their racial identity. According to Derman-Sparks and Edwards (2019: 16),

> [s]ome teachers and parents are not sure they should encourage children to 'notice' and learn about differences among people. They may think that it is best to teach only about how people are the same, worrying that talking about difference causes prejudice. While well intentioned, this concern arises from a mistaken notion about the sources of bias.

It assumes that recognising difference is wrong in and of itself, rather than the judgements we place on the cause or value of difference. As educators, we should 'assume that differences within and between groups are normal and desirable' and strive to share this understanding with the children that they teach and the representations we embed within our settings (MacNaughton and Hughes, 2011: 199).

Derman-Sparks and Edwards (2019: 16) are very clear that 'differences between people do not create the bias… Children learn prejudice from prejudice – not from learning about human diversity'. Discussion is therefore a vitally important strategy in an educator's professional practice to tackle prejudice and create meaningful opportunities that help children to develop a positive understanding of their own and others' racial identity. As educators, we should strive to be role models for children, countering damaging stereotypical attitudes and problematic behaviours towards difference. We should deal with children's questions about race fairly, openly, and honestly.

How effectively educators respond to children's questions about the differences that they see around them will ultimately teach them how to respond. In continuous provision, educators can provide children with access to tools that enable them to meaningfully depict different skin tones (e.g., with felt tips, paints, pencils, and crayons) so that they are better able to represent themselves literally and symbolically. Many mainstream and independent brands have developed inclusive resources to fill the long-standing void in the representation of darker skin tones in Western societies. For example, in 2020 Crayola introduced their *Colours of the World Crayons*, which give children the freedom to draw what they see and how they identify, whilst award-winning brands, such as Little Omo, provide a range of educational toys, from puzzles to flashcards, that teach children about diverse cultural representation.

These resources not only open up opportunities to talk about race but can also give educators an insight into how children feel about themselves. If educators do not take everyday opportunities to talk to children about similarities and differences, then children may learn that being different is not favourable. This will have an effect on children's sense of self-identity and their self-worth.

Exercise

You can do this exercise as a group, with others in your educational setting, or on your own as a form of self-reflection. You'll need a piece of paper and a pen. Please write down the *first* answer that you think of.

1. Close your eyes and think of someone you consider to be beautiful. Hold on to that image.
   Who did you see?
2. Now, take a minute to close your eyes and think of someone you consider to be successful. Hold on to that image.
   Who did you see?
3. Think of a princess, an astronaut, an engineer, a scientist, a doctor, a judge, or a head teacher.
   Who did you see?

Reflecting on this exercise, did the people or characters you thought of have anything in common? How many of them were White? How many of them were people of colour?

Different kinds of hair

Young children also notice differences in hair texture and the types of hairstyles that their friends, families, and those they see represented in books or on TV have. They may ask questions, such as, 'Why is Daniel's hair big and bouncy?', or 'Why does Aunty Delicia wear a wig?' They may wonder why people in their families have different colours, lengths, and textures of hair, or why they all have the same type of hair and how it can change. They may make negative comments, with terms like 'messy', 'slimy', or 'greasy' used to describe other people's hair. Or you may see them reach out and touch someone else's hair in a bid to better understand it.

Having dolls with European, Afro-Caribbean, and Asian hair, or books that talk positively about different hair textures (such as Rochelle Humes' debut book *The Mega Magic Hair Swap!*), can help children to learn about similarities and differences, but these alone are not enough. Educators should actively consider how to give children developmentally appropriate information to support and embed these resources. This needs to be done both proactively and on an ad hoc basis, in response to potentially challenging conversations or behaviours that you may witness.

The key is to meet the child at the stage of development that they are at, without judgement. Asika (2020: 182) gives several examples of how you can do this:

> Ask [a] child if they can come up with three kind, positive and empowering words to describe their own hair and someone else's. See if they can switch out terms like 'greasy' or 'bushy' for happier words like 'smooth' or 'free'.

Or why not ask '[w]hat comments about their own hair would make them happy, and what might make them feel bad?'. Asika (2020: 183–184) goes on to emphasise the importance of teaching children boundaries and consent – children need to know that touching someone's hair (or any other part of them) without their explicit consent is never okay. There's nothing wrong with being inquisitive but, as Asika explains, we must always act with kindness and compassion.

For young children to grow up to be confident and self-assured citizens of the world, educators should also consider how we can encourage young children to be *proud* of their hair because a child's hair can be a cornerstone of their identity or an important part of how they express themselves. A quick Google search of the phrases 'professional hair' and 'unprofessional hair' will tell you all you need to know about the persistent discrimination and racism levied at people with Afro-Caribbean hair in the Western world. If you have grown up with European hair in a Western country, it can sometimes be hard to understand how a child's hair can affect their sense of self-worth because it may have never been something that you have had to question. After all, no three-year-old is going to be Googling professional or unprofessional hairstyles, are they? Well, maybe not. But the world around them communicates value-laden examples that support the inherently racist perception that Black hair equals ugly and unsuccessful, whilst White hair equals beauty and success, and these messages become internalised. The impact that this can have on young children should not be underestimated.

In 2017, when describing her inspiration to start embracing her naturally curly hair, TV personality Rochelle Humes wrote on Instagram:

> My 4 year old little girl Alaia has been telling me for a while that she doesn't like her curly hair. At first (as us Mums do) I didn't think it was a big deal. Once I realised this wasn't a phase I asked why she didn't like her curls. It broke my heart when she told me it was because she didn't look like a Princess. And I quote: 'I don't Mummy because Elsa and Rapunzel have long straight hair'.
>
> (Humes, 2017)

It's not just children that internalise these messages. As adults and as educators, we do too, and our own views about racial difference can be just as damaging for children as the messages they internalise from the media. In 2020, mixed-race teenager Ruby Williams hit the headlines after repeatedly being sent home by her teachers in the UK. The teachers argued that her natural Afro hair was 'too big'. The school policy dictated that to be permitted on school grounds, their policy dictated that her hair 'must be of a reasonable size and length' (Bubola, 2022). Ruby's family mounted a legal challenge, which led to new guidance being issued to schools in England, Scotland, and Wales in 2022 to ensure their policies on hair are not unlawfully discriminatory.

Whilst Ruby is older than the children that form the focus of this book, her story is a powerful example of the impact that the individual racial bias of a teacher and the institutional racial bias of a school can have on a young person, particularly when it comes to their sense of belonging. For no reason other than choosing to wear her hair naturally, Ruby was denied access to educational provision and instructed to dilute her Blackness in order to belong. Aside from raising a vital question about who decides what is 'reasonable' and what is not, Ruby's experience shows us what happens when racial bias and prejudice are left unchecked. Learning how to celebrate, manage, and care for different hair types can have a massive impact on the development of self-esteem and identity within a child.

Reflective questions

- What representations exist within the learning environment that you work in?
- Does your setting have examples of similar hair or hairstyles to the children attending?
  - Are the representations of the majority or the minority?
  - Are they positive or negative?
  - What message(s) does this send to the children in my care?

Case study – not our hair

Adapted from Louis, S. and Betteridge, H. (2020) *Unconscious Bias in the Observation, Assessment and Planning Process.* Foundation Stage Forum.

In a small rural village preschool, two sisters of mixed heritage attended an all-White setting. One day the staff set up a role play area as a hairdressing salon. It had all sorts of mirrors, brushes, shower caps, hairdryers, and product packages. The sisters raced into the salon with their friends but very quickly came out quiet and despondent. When the educator asked them what was wrong, they replied, 'There's nothing for us'.

When their mum came to pick them up, the educator had a discussion with her about the children's lack of engagement. To facilitate the discussion, the educator took the mum into the role play area. The mum explained that the girls used Afro combs and different types of products in their hair. She kindly gave the setting some resources to use, and it sparked lots of positive conversations with the other children about differences in hair and differences between people in general.

From this discussion, the educator understood that she had not represented the girls' culture well enough. The educator recognised that she would need to gather more information from the parents in order to counter her Eurocentric practice that had initially unintentionally excluded the girls. The two girls were not being difficult or challenging because they didn't want to engage, they simply could not see how they fit in with the resources provided. It is also important to remember that not all children will have the experience of going to the hairdresser – for example, for religious reasons children, including those that are Rastafarian and Sikh, may choose not to have their hair cut.

Reflective questions

- Do the resources in your setting reflect a range of different cultural and religious practices?
- Do they centre the stories and/or experiences of children of colour?

It is only by observing and listening to children attentively and with an open mind that we begin to avoid bias. Being open to how children learn, their interests, and how they think and solve problems will help us to value them as unique individuals. This case study highlights how educators can more consciously organise the learning environment to build on children's cultural practices, thereby helping them to make it part of their thinking about themselves. The physical learning environment sends powerful messages about what is acceptable. The more inclusive our environment, the more likely it is that children will come to believe that their attributes are of great value, and this will have a positive impact on the development of their racial identity. However, if young children are frequently exposed to resources that are unfamiliar and fail to represent them, they may not engage with them at all, curtailing their opportunities for learning.

The power of books

In this chapter, we have alluded to the power of books to help children build a positive sense of identity, and their ability to act as a valuable jumping-off point for discussions about similarities and differences. But not all books are created equal.

Reflective question

When was the last time you conducted an audit of the books in your setting?

For decades, study after study has shown examples of children's books playing up to harmful stereotypes, representing cultures inaccurately or confining ethnic minority characters to the background, with little to no agency or voice (Edmonds, 1986; Mendoza and Reese, 2001; Hughes-Hassell and Cox, 2010). Indeed, all too often we see Whiteness framed as something positive, portraying 'innocence' or 'purity', whilst the villains that we read about are given darker features (e.g., Scar in *The Lion King*), with children quickly learning to associate Blackness as something to be fearful of. That is to say if the books we read even choose to represent anything other than Whiteness at all.

Flicking through the pages of children's books, it is clear to see that the stories we surround young people with predominantly show the world through a White lens. More than that, they tend to promote a very specific version of Whiteness as the ideal. As Derman-Sparks and Edwards (2019: 7) describe, 'too many early childhood materials focus on children and families who resemble the stereotypes of American culture as it is most commonly depicted – middle class, White suburban, able-bodied, English-speaking, mother and father (nuclear) family – as if these were the only types of children and families we work with'.

This is not just an American problem – the same is true within other Western cultures. In 2020, the Centre for Literacy in Primary Education (CLPE) published a UK study, which concluded that only seven per cent of children's books published in the UK between 2017 to 2019 featured characters of colour. Worst still, only five per cent had Black, Asian, or ethnic minority protagonists, despite children of an ethnic minority background making up 33.5% of the UK primary school population (CLPE, 2020). Two years later, after what CLPE referred to as 'a considerable effort and commitment…to improving the volume and quality of representative and inclusive literature', they found that 20% of children's picture books featured characters of colour, with nine per cent featuring a main character from a 'racially minoritised background' (CLPE, 2022).

Whilst there is a lot to be said for the momentum and progress that has been made in diversifying the stories available on our bookshelves, there is still more work to be done. Four key points stand out:

- First, despite a concerted effort, children's picture books still underrepresent people of colour.
- Second, although representation is on the up, progress has been much slower when it comes to increasing the presence of main characters of colour. This matters because children deserve to see themselves as the heroes of their own story, rather than being confined to being a sidekick of others. For children of colour to be able to meaningfully explore their identity and the world around them through the pages they read, we need authentic multi-dimensional characters of colour that are central to the narrative.

Table 4.1 Percentage of Total Books Published Featuring Ethnic Minority Main Characters in the UK

	2017	2018	2019	2020	2021
Arab	0.1%	0.2%	0.2%	0.2%	Less than 0.1%
Asian	0.5%	0.14%	0.3%	0.7%	0.9%
Black	1%	1%	2%	2.2%	4.6%
Chinese	0.1%	0.1%	0.2%	0.3%	0.3%
Mixed Heritage	0.2%	0.3%	0.9%	0.8%	0.7%
Other	0.3%	0.3%	0.3%	0.5%	3%

Source: CLPE Reflecting Race Study 2020 and CLPE Reflecting Race Study 2022

- Third, whilst the CLPE notes that 'growth in presence is only as meaningful as the quality of the portrayals', their studies of race representation in UK children's picture books do not offer a quantitative insight into the quality of the portrayals in the books they have analysed (2022: 9). They do, however, provide an indication that the picture is not rosy. Through the process of reviewing recently published material, their team observed 'that the range of presence [that characters of colour have] continues to be varied. At times the presence is problematic and poorly executed and at others it is too insignificant to have any real weight' (CLPE, 2022: 12). This gap in the data makes it hard to discern if the increase we have seen in representation over the last few years will truly help to shift the dial. After all, the words and images ensnared within each page of a book have as much potential to inflict damage to a child's self-identity as they do to build a child up.
- Fourth, the headline statistics hide a varied picture of progress amongst different ethnicities, and that is without getting into the diverse array of cultures and experiences within each of the ethnicities listed below (see Table 4.1).

An image tells a thousand words

On closer inspection, many historically well-loved children's books include problematic portrayals of race. Take *The Ugly Duckling* – there are now many variations of the original fairy tale created by Hans Christian Andersen, but the messages within their pages often tell the same story. On a warm summer day, a mother duck excitedly waits for her eggs to hatch. When they do, she sees a 'big, ugly gray one' (Andersen, 1843). Cutting a long story short, rejected by his mother and siblings for being different, the ugly duckling goes in search of somewhere he fits in. As he grows up, he becomes a beautiful, white swan. Gone are his 'dirty' 'gray' feathers, considered throughout the story to be 'ugly and offensive' (Andersen, 1843). In their place are snowy white feathers. Magically he is finally accepted by all the great swans around him. The key lesson we're told: 'Being born in a duck nest does not matter, if only you are hatched from a swan's egg' (Andersen, 1843). But what if you're not hatched from a swan's egg?

Ironically, The Ugly Duckling is often hailed as a wonderful children's story that teaches you not to judge a book by its cover and to accept someone for all the qualities they possess. It's even used on Racism No Way, a website developed by the Australian Government to promote anti-racism in schools, as an exercise for helping children develop an understanding of fairness, respect, inclusion, and exclusion in social groups (New South Wales Department for Education, 2000). Whilst the story may show the pain that exclusion can cause, several important questions have arguably been overlooked. Why are the duckling's distinctive grey feathers, which make him noticeably darker in his appearance, the source of his ugliness? Why do they cause 'offence'? And why is he only accepted and considered beautiful once his feathers become white? What messages does this teach children of all races about their self-worth?

In 2019, British supermarket chain, Waitrose, was forced to apologise and temporarily remove a trio of chocolate ducklings from sale during Easter. The ducklings, comprised of milk, white, and dark chocolate, were named 'fluffy', 'crispy', and 'ugly' respectively. By choosing to name the darkest duckling 'ugly', shoppers quickly labelled the product 'racist' (Zatat, 2019). Yet during the research we conducted for this book, we found it near impossible to find the same criticisms of racism levied at the story of The Ugly Duckling, despite the labels being the same. Rivera (2017) explains:

[t]his kind of subconscious white-washing happens frequently in the media. The connotations behind things are not noticed because it is extremely normal in our world to see people change, especially physically in order to fit in with society's beauty standards.

Going further, she notes that the implicit messages within *The Ugly Duckling* can be dangerous precisely due to the way that our brains assimilate information as fact over time, with children learning that Whiteness is the ideal state of being and with it comes acceptance and beauty (Rivera, 2017).

The tacit acceptance we give to stories that place Whiteness as something to be desired is not unique, nor are the number of problematic stories we have grown to accept. The messages we are taught as children are often internalised and become deeply embedded in our unconscious minds as the norm from which all things are judged. Given this, it is perhaps unsurprising that it took over 80 years for six Dr. Seuss books to be questioned, before the decision was taken to finally stop reproducing them in 2022 because of their racist and insensitive imagery.

In our work, we should strive to be sensitive to how the stories we teach may be interpreted. We should be judicious in our choice of educational materials, bringing in voices and stories written by people of colour, and encourage discussion about the meaning and messages of stories we teach.

Curating choice

Books and stories clearly have an important place in children's lives. The stories that children hear and the images that they see will influence how they see themselves. If children see books where representations of people who look like them are depicted as ugly, violent, aggressive, and underachieving, they will internalise these messages about themselves. This can be detrimental to their racial identity and self-image. Children of colour need to see positive representations of people who look like them to enable them to think that they too can be successful. This includes having dual language books and books that represent positive attitudes to diversity. All educators should reflect on the gaps in their provision, as the impact of children not seeing people like themselves and their families represented in books and in the environment can be a key barrier to helping them develop a positive sense of identity.

The library of books available within an early years setting should be carefully curated. This means doing your research, being open to reflection, and open to challenge. Children should never be made to feel that their race, religion, ethnicity, or culture is undesirable, as this will affect their sense of belonging and how they perceive themselves. As educators, we have to understand the impact that unchallenged stereotypes and racial caricatures can have on how children perceive themselves and others. When schools and early years settings embrace and value a diversity of cultures and provide children with learning materials and experiences that are culturally sensitive and responsible, children are far more likely to feel confident and self-assured in themselves and be less fearful or distrusting of difference. As Professor Bishop (1990) argues,

> [w]hen children cannot find themselves reflected in the books they read, or when the images they see are distorted, negative, or laughable, they learn a powerful lesson about how they are devalued in the society of which they are a part. Our classrooms need to be placed where all the children from all the cultures that make up the salad bowl of [our] society can find their mirrors.

However, this impact is not just felt by children of colour. As Bishop (1990) goes on to explain:

> Children from dominant social groups have always found their mirrors in books, but they, too, have suffered from the lack of availability of books about others... They need books that will help them understand the multicultural nature of the world they live in, and their place as a member of just one group, as well as their connections to all other humans. In this country, where racism is still one of the major unresolved social problems, books may be one of the few places where children who are socially isolated and insulated from the larger world may meet people unlike themselves. If they see only reflections of themselves, they will grow up with an exaggerated sense of their own importance and value in the world a dangerous ethnocentrism.

Repeated exposure to meaningful examples of different races, religions, cultures, and ethnicities is therefore key to not only developing a positive self-identity, but to reducing prejudice amongst young children. This finding is supported by Vogel et al. (2012) who found that children are less likely to hold and display bias towards different racial groups if they have greater exposure to other races and Lane (2008) who suggests that bias may decrease with better representation of marginalised groups.

The representations that children are exposed to in books found in the learning environment should be taken seriously by educators. They have an important role to play in providing children with a rich learning environment, guiding them, and helping them to develop their self-identity and respect for others. Stories are not just myths and legends; they are transformative. They have the power to shape and inspire young minds, making it vital that educators look closely at the materials they have available.

Exercise

Conduct an audit of the books in your setting and consider the following questions:

- What storylines do they promote?
- What is presented as 'good' or 'bad'? Who are the heroes and villains?
- How is power exercised in the narrative? Who got their own way, and how?
- Who is the main character? Who is on the sidelines?
- What messages does it convey about relationships between people?
- Is it presented through a White lens? Does it promote an 'us' versus 'them' rhetoric?
- Do they contain harmful stereotypes, cultural inaccuracies, or loaded words?
- What implicit and explicit messages do they send to young children about race?

Paving the way for change

All educators have a pedagogical responsibility to think about how we promote racial equality and equity for the children and families that we work with. This means regularly planning meaningful activities and reviewing the resources in our settings to ensure we give children developmentally appropriate information about different racial and cultural groups, while being clear that, although some people may be different, no one is superior because of the colour of their skin.

However, in providing space for discussion, we must be wary of falling into the trap of thinking that developmentally appropriate conversations need to be structured around heavily watered-down versions of reality. Children understand far more than we give them credit for and without accurate and honest discussions about race, the children we teach will leave our care ill-equipped to navigate a society predicated on institutional racism. Not only will they be unable to identify it in all its forms, but they will also be less likely to be able to effectively address and counter racism when it presents itself. Indeed, as Hirschfeld (2008: 49) argues, it is vital that children are 'presented with appropriate – not dumbed down – descriptions of the nature and scope of structural racial inequity' by educators, as it is through this knowledge that they are able to 'appreciate the group nature of racial prejudice' and the ways in which racism manifests. Children need to understand that racism is a societal problem, not just a problem created by a few individuals. At times these discussions may be painful and uncomfortable, but silence will not generate progress. It will simply leave people of colour to carry the burden and pain of tackling racism on their own.

To have the desired effect, our discussions about race and racism with children should therefore be frequent and meaningful, with opportunities provided for Black and Brown voices to share their truth. And our settings should seek to proactively represent the beauty of diversity and inclusion with diverse role models for all children to see. Using all of the tools at our disposal, we should do our due diligence to curate a pedagogical approach that actively counters racial discrimination and prejudice, and empowers all children to love the skin they are in.

The learning environment children are placed in has an essential role to play in determining what they learn about themselves and their cultural practices, what is valued and accepted, and what is not. Let's not forget the role we play in creating it.

Recommended reading for children

The following list aims to provide you with a collection of books with positive representations of children of a range of different cultures, ethnicities, and religions. It is not an exhaustive list and we strongly recommend conducting your own research to find books that meet the interests and needs of the children in your setting.

- *A World for Me and You: Where Everyone is Welcome* by Uju Asika
- *Amy Wu and the Perfect Bao* by Kat Zhang
- *Black: The Many Wonders of My World* by Nancy Johnson James
- *Everyone Loves Lunchtime but Zia* by Jenny Liao
- *Eyes That Kiss in the Corners* by Joanna Ho
- *Hates of Faith* by Medeia Cohan
- *I'm a Girl* by Yasmeen Ismail
- *Julian Is a Mermaid* by Jessica Love
- *M Is for Melanin* by Tiffany Rose
- *Meesha Makes Friends* by Tom Percival
- *My Skin, Your Skin* by Laura Henry-Allain MBE
- *My Uncle and Me* by Ashley Hinds
- *Ossiri and the Bala Mengro* by Richard O'Neill and Katharine Quarmby
- *Ravi's Roar* by Tom Percival
- *Riley Can Be Anything* by Davina Hamilton
- *Ruby's Worry* by Tom Percival
- *Skin Again* by Bell Hooks
- *The Many Colours of Harpreet Singh* by Supriya Kelkar
- *The Mega Magic Hair Swap!* by Rochelle Humes
- *The Proudest Blue* by Ibtihaj Muhammad and S.K. Ali
- *Yokki and the Parno Gry* by Richard O'Neill and Katharine Quarmby

For more recommendations, follow @booksfordiversity on Instagram.

References

Andersen, H.C. (1843) *The Ugly Duckling: Original Translation*. Available at: http://visitandersen.com/fairy-tales/ugly-duckling.

Asika, U. (2020) *Bringing up Race: How to Raise a Kind Child in a Prejudiced World*. Great Britain: Yellow Kite.

Belli, B. (2020) 'It's Never Too Early to Talk with Children about Race'. *Yale News*. Available at: https://news.yale.edu/2020/06/15/its-never-too-early-talk-children -about-race.

Bishop, R.S. (1990) 'Mirrors, Windows and Sliding Glass Doors'. *Perspectives: Choosing and Using Books for the Classroom*, 6(3). Available at: https://scenicregional.org/wp-content/uploads/2017/08/Mirrors-Windows-and-Sliding-Glass-Doors.pdf.

Bubola, E. (2022) 'U.K. Tells Schools They Can't Ban Afro Hairstyles'. *New York Times*, 27 October. Available at: https://www.nytimes.com/2022/10/27/world/europe/uk-schools-afro-hair.html.

Centre of Literacy in Primary Education (2020) *Reflecting Realities: Survey of Ethnic Representation within UK Children's Literature 2019*. Available at: https://clpe.org.uk/system/files/CLPE%20Reflecting%20Realities%202020.pdf.

Centre of Literacy in Primary Education (2022) *Reflecting Realities: Survey of Ethnic Representation within UK Children's Literature 2017–2021*. Available at: https://clpe.org.uk/system/files/2022-11/CLPE%20Reflecting%20Reality%202022%20WEB_0.pdf.

Derman-Sparks, L. and Edwards, J.O. (2019) *Anti-Bias Education for Young Children & Ourselves*. Washington, DC: National Association of Educators of Young Children.

Edmonds, L. (1986) 'The Treatment of Race in Picture Books for Young Children'. *Book Research Quarterly*, 2(3), pp. 30–41.

Hirschfeld, L.A. (2008) 'Children's Developing Conceptions of Race'. In S.M. Quintana and C. McKown (eds.) *Handbook of Race, Racism, and the Developing Child*. Hoboken, NJ: John Wiley & Sons, pp. 37–54.

Hughes-Hassell, S. and Cox, E.J. (2010) 'Inside Board Books: Representations of People of Color'. *Library Quarterly*, 80(3), pp. 211–230.

Humes, R. (2017) '#GoingBackToMyRoots My Four Year Old Little Girl Alaia Has Been Telling Me for a While That She Doesn't Like Her Curly Hair […]'. *Instagram*, 13 December. Available at: https://www.instagram.com/p/Bco51NqhWhk/?igshid=YmMyMTA2M2Y%3D.

Humes, R. (2019) *The Mega Magic Hair Swap!* London: Studio Press.

Katz, P.A. and Kofkin, J.A. (1997) 'Race, Gender and Young Children'. In S.S. Luthar, J.A. Burack, D. Cicchetti and J.R. Weisz (eds.) *Developmental Psychopathology: Perspectives on Adjustment, Risk, and Disorder*. Cambridge: Cambridge University Press, pp. 51–74.

Kelly, D.J., Quinn, P.C., Slater, A.M., Lee, K., Gibson, A., Smith, M., Ge, L. and Pascalis, O. (2005) 'Three-Month-Olds, But Not Newborns, Prefer Own-Race Faces'. *Developmental Science*, 8, pp. 31–36.

Lane, J. (2008) *Young Children and Racial Justice*. London: National Children's Bureau.

Louis, S. (2022) 'Should We Talk to Children About Race?'. In A. Thomas (ed.) *Representation Matters. Becoming an Anti-racist Educator*. London: Bloomsbury, pp. 62–65.

Louis, S. and Betteridge, H. (2020) 'Unconscious Bias in the Observation, Assessment and Planning Process'. *Foundation Stage Forum*, 17 November. Available at: https://eyfs.info/articles.html/general/unconscious-bias-in-the-observation-assessment-and-planning-process-r338/.

MacNaughton, G. and Hughes, P. (2011) *Parents and Professionals in Early Childhood Settings*. Berkshire: Open University Press.

Mendoza, J. and Reese, D. (2001) 'Examining Multicultural Picture Books for the Early Childhood Classroom: Possibilities and Pitfalls'. *Early Childhood Research and Practice*, 3(2), pp. 1–31.

New South Wales Department for Education. (2000) 'K.10: Traditional Tales'. *Racism No Way*. Available at: https://racismnoway.com.au/teaching-resources/anti-prejudice-activities/kindergarten/traditional-tales/.

Rivera, N.G. (2017) 'Is the Ugly Duckling Narrative Problematic?' *Affinity Magazine*. Available at: https://affinitymagazine.us/2017/03/26/is-the-ugly-duckling-narrative-problematic/.

United Nations (1989) *Convention on the Rights of the Child*. UN General Assembly Document A/RES/44/2. New York: United Nations.

Vandenbroeck, M. (2008) 'The Challenge for Early Childhood Education and Care'. In L. Brooker and M. Woodhead (eds.) *Developing Positive Identities: Diversity and Young Children. Early Childhood in Focus 3*. Milton Keynes: Open University.

Vogel, M., Monesson, A. and Scott, L.S. (2012) 'Building Biases in Infancy: The Influence of Race on Face and Voice Emotion Matching'. *Developmental Science*, 15(3), pp. 359–375.

Zatat, N. (2019) 'Waitrose Apologises after "Ugly" Dark Chocolate Duckling Sparks Race Row'. *Indy 100*, 9 April. Available at: https://racismnoway.com.au/teaching-resources/anti-prejudice-activities/kindergarten/traditional-tales/.

5
Developing an inclusive learning environment
Stella Louis and Hannah Betteridge

When was the last time you critically examined your setting, or encouraged others of a different background to yourself to do the same?

The physical learning environment has a significant impact on children's cognitive development. From the resources that educators make available, to the flow and layout of the spaces that we design, educators have a powerful opportunity to support, extend, and plan for children's interests, inspiring their imaginations and igniting continuous learning about themselves and the world around them. That is why supporters of the internationally renowned Reggio Emilia approach to education refer to the environment as 'the third teacher' – with the first two being a child's parents and carers (Cadwell, 1997: 5).

Without due diligence, there is a danger that we can unwittingly place Whiteness at the centre of the learning environments we construct in Western societies by reinforcing Whiteness as the default and everything else as the 'other'. This can significantly disadvantage the personal, social, and emotional development of children of colour in our settings. It is therefore incumbent on every educator to understand, recognise, and act when we see this occur.

Perhaps unsurprisingly, the quality of the physical environment directly correlates to the quality of practice (Manning-Morton, 2004). As a general rule, settings should be welcoming, cosy, and representative of the children in our care, their families, and the wider community. The layout and materials should be carefully considered, promoting opportunities for independent learning, collaboration, and exploration. They should engage all a child's senses and support their individual needs, including the positive development of their self-identity with respect to their race and culture.

DOI: 10.4324/9781003251149-7

Exercise

Take a moment to imagine your setting. With a piece of paper and a pen, draw a rough plan of the setting that you work in, listing the resources on offer within each area.

Step 1: Thinking about the observations you have made in the past month, note down how the children in your setting have interacted with the environment around them. Consider whether every child has interacted with their surroundings equally. Ask yourself what this might tell you about whether their interests have been represented.

Step 2: Now imagine your setting through the eyes of a Black Caribbean, Mexican, Polish, Turkish, South East Asian, or Indian child. As you walk around your setting, consider how (if at all) their racial and cultural identity and interests have been represented. Ask yourself:

- Are different races and cultures represented in your setting in an authentic and meaningful way?
- Does the home corner include foods, utensils, and personal care items (e.g., hair care) that they use at home?
- Does the sensory play area include fabrics and materials from their culture?
- Can they see themselves, their family, or their local community reflected on the shelves of the book corner?
- Do the activities set up in the creative/art station allow them to explore their racial and cultural identity?
- Does the music corner include musical instruments or songs that they will recognise?
- What might your answers to the question above tell them about the value of (a) their interests, and (b) their racial and cultural identity?

Using the plan that you drew of your setting at the start of this exercise, highlight the areas that are most inclusive and those that, upon reflection, may be exclusive. As you read through this chapter, consider what upgrades you could make to ensure the physical environment supports all children to thrive, and how you could create regular safe spaces to gather the views of the children in your setting and their families.

The historical context: assimilation vs anti-racist approaches to education

The physical learning environment of educational settings has a particularly significant role to play in championing a multicultural and anti-racist pedagogical approach that celebrates difference, whilst also tackling inequality. However, throughout the course of history, the learning environment has been used as a tool to promote assimilation into a dominant Western culture, which is primed as superior, in an attempt to 'manage' and 'constrain' 'problem' populations (Shain, 2013: 63; Grosvenor, 1997). Given how receptive young children are to their environment, this is a worrying trend.

> **Assimilation** can be defined as the expectation that minority groups must 'abandon their cultural norms and practices in favour of those of the host society' (Shain, 2013: 63). By contrast, **anti-racist** approaches to education start from the perspective that a plurality of races and cultures is desirable. It goes beyond the idea that simply not being racist is enough and can be defined as the *active* opposition to racism and promotion of racial equality.

Unfortunately, it is still easy to see the roots of assimilationist policies present within educational settings today. You can see it in predominately White book corners (see Chapter 4) and home corners, in the music we teach (see Chapter 6), and in our assessment practices (Coard, 2021). By building our societies and educational systems on the principle that Whiteness is superior, we have placed an extraordinary amount of pressure on children of colour, their families, and their communities to reject or hide parts of themselves, such as their home language, traditional clothing, food, or skin colour, to fit in with the 'norm' and be accepted. Far from nurturing a positive sense of self, this can make children of colour feel different or inferior. This pressure can come from a wide range of sources, including: an educator's bias, the creation of a monolithic environment that centres Whiteness above all else, and a curriculum that perpetuates support for the Empire and colonisation based on a fallacy that Western societies needed to educate and civilise other cultures to somehow save them from savagery. Indeed, the very 'problem of assimilation is that it demands of the person the rejection of his or her present self in order to become a part of the majority – like everyone else' (Bruce, 1987: 150). This can be hugely damaging to the value, or lack thereof, that a child places on themselves, their culture, and their heritage.

In the UK, the very development of the National Curriculum 'was considered by some of those responsible for its drafting to be the means by which a common UK identity was to be fostered among pupils' (Department for Education and Skills, 2007: 26). It was a structural tool to squash linguistic and cultural diversity – both of which were perceived to be threatening and 'undesirable', particularly in large quantities (Commonwealth Immigrants Advisory Council, 1964: para. 25). Although it is easy to think that times have moved on, the structures that underpin educational systems around the world are well entrenched and have remained relatively stable. Too often, we see diversity, equity, and inclusion presented as a tick box exercise or an add-on, rather than an essential principle that should inform our practice. This can lead to shallow and tokenistic portrayals of different races and cultures that reinforce one child's culture as 'normal' and anything else as 'foreign' or 'exotic'; thereby increasing the risk of non-dominant cultures being devalued or misunderstood (McGeary, 2021).

Developing an inclusive learning environment that champions an anti-racist approach to education requires educators to critically examine their surroundings and give due regard and value to each child's individuality, family, race, religion, abilities, cultural practices, and linguistic background. These characteristics have a substantial influence on how children develop emotionally, socially, and linguistically and should therefore inform our approach. The type and effectiveness of the learning that takes place in educational settings will be determined by how educators organise the learning environment. If appropriate racial, cultural, and linguistic experiences are not incorporated into the environment, it makes it harder for every child to show educators what they know and can do. It is only when educators are open to learning about children's cultural values that they can help children to see themselves reflected in the environment. In every setting, educators should strive to ensure the physical environment is racially and culturally diverse. It should be responsive to children's needs, supporting them to express themselves across all areas of the curriculum and creating a sense of belonging.

The importance of the environment cannot be overstated. As renowned educator and philosopher Maria Montessori noted:

> Adults admire their environment; they can remember it and think about it – but a child absorbs it. The things he sees are not just remembered; they form part of his soul. He incarnates in himself all in the world about him that his eyes see and his ears hear.

(2016: 56)

As educators, we all carry a responsibility to ensure that children can see themselves represented in their surroundings to feel loved, valued, and respected.

My home or your home?

As young children navigate our educational settings, they learn about themselves through their play and explorations – about who they are and what they might become as they rehearse different roles. They will imitate and pretend. As Froebel (1887) argues, children have a need to express their inner lives in their outward activity to make sense of their own first-hand experiences. Through your observations, you will notice that their pretend play is brimming full of information about how they understand relationships, power dynamics, and the values they have absorbed. If children's home lives and daily experiences are absent from the learning environment, we inadvertently narrow the learning opportunities available for children to make sense of their identity and the world around them.

What is included in and excluded from the home corner can therefore send children hidden messages about themselves, their sociocultural norms, and that of others. Through their environment, young children pick up coded messages about what is desirable and what is not. In this way, children are influenced by both the environment and the people that they interact with. They will learn from every interaction and reaction, and these interactions shape how young children begin to perceive themselves.

Case study – making fufu

Two-year-old Emi is Black and of Nigerian heritage. She can frequently be found preparing food in the home corner; pretending to boil water and mixing and mashing her ingredients. Emi always begins by pretending to clean the kitchen, wiping surfaces, and putting things away in the cupboard. Next, she sets the table up with a ball of dough on a plate and a small bowl with water. Emi pretends to get the doll ready for dinner by putting a bib on it. She sits the doll on her lap and begins to break off small pieces of play dough, dips them into the bowl, then places them in the doll's mouth with her fingers. After each mouthful she wipes the dolly's mouth saying, 'Mmmmm, you like fufu don't you'.[1] Emi insists that the fufu will make the baby strong and full.

- What does this example show about Emi's cultural norms?
- How might Western cultural norms about eating with cutlery affect Emi's perception of her cultural identity?
- How might you support Emi's development following this observation using the tools available in your setting?
- How could you include the making of fufu in your planning and involve other children?
- Thinking about Emi's knowledge about how to make fufu, how could you help Emi and the other children in your setting make connections with each other, whilst normalising difference?

Incorporating children's home culture and family lives into the learning environment can support them to develop a positive view of themselves and provide meaningful learning opportunities for children of different races and cultures to learn about the experiences of others, creating a more inclusive and accurate world view. As educators, we need to be willing to position ourselves as learners and regularly seek to expand our knowledge of different cultures to be able to effectively guide children as they navigate their way through issues relating to race and identity. One of the ways we can do this is by developing close partnerships with parents, carers, and families. We can sensitively and respectfully ask what foods they eat at home, what utensils or products (e.g., bamboo steamers, chopsticks, a pestle and mortar, spices, etc.) they use, and ask about the most important aspects of their culture within their home lives. We can also invite parents and carers into the learning environment regularly to talk about how well it reflects their home life and their child's interests, making space for them to offer suggestions to create an open and respectful dialogue between families and educators. This is an essential foundation for the creation of an effective and inclusive physical learning environment for those in our care.

Case study – Josh's chicken

Four-year-olds Josh and Niall were observed playing in the home corner. Josh is Black and of Jamaican heritage and Niall is mixed-race; his mum is White British, and his dad is Brazilian. They were busy pretending to season chicken and fry it. The educator, Nathan, encouraged them to write or draw the ingredients that they were using to help support their learning. Noticing how much fun Josh and Niall were having, more children wandered over into the home corner and added more spices to the mix.

At the end of the day, Nathan sent an email to the parents and/or carers of every child, asking them to write down or take a photo of their favourite dish to make at home, and planned a shopping trip for the following week with the children. Nathan printed out all the pictures and made a colourful display entitled 'our favourite foods' with flags underneath the title of each dish. Before heading out to the shops, Nathan empowered each of the children to help decide what they are going to cook that day and select the ingredients that they would need for their recipe, using the display board as a catalyst for inspiration. The children decided to make Josh's jerk chicken first.

Whilst out shopping, Niall explained that he was scared to touch the chilli. Nathan reassured him that chillies are only hot when they are cut open or when you bite into them. As they walked around the aisles, Josh told Nathan and Niall a story about when his dad rubbed his eye after cutting a chilli and it made him cry. This started a discussion amongst the children about chillies and how hot it would make their chicken. Josh announced that he did not want to use chillies. Instead, he wanted the other ingredients you need to make jerk chicken, including pepper, nutmeg, and garlic. All the children agreed.

When they got back to school, the children were involved in grating, cutting, pressing, and sprinkling the different herbs. They talked about the different smells and flavours, and Josh told them that nutmeg grew inside a yellow fruit on the leaves of a tree in Jamaica. As the food was cooking, Josh described a recent trip he took to see his grandparents in the summer, recounting how 'hot' and 'green' Jamaica was. Josh talked about some of the other food he enjoyed eating at home, including plantain and yam, and Nathan encouraged all the children to share stories about their favourite foods too.

Over the following weeks, Nathan collected empty spice jars and product boxes from the parents and/or carers of children who attended the setting. He created a mini spice rack in the home corner to display them all, enabling the children to continue to explore different cultures and foods at their leisure. He also involved the children in an activity to expand the display board and included drawings of different types of vegetables and fruits that you find around the world to prompt further discussions and tasting sessions.

Reflecting on this case study, ask yourself:

- How did Nathan use food to introduce the children to new cultures?
- Has Nathan effectively made exploration of cultural identities part of his continuous learning provision? If yes, how has he done so? If no, what else do you think he could have done in this scenario?
- Thinking beyond the home corner, how else could Nathan build on this activity and meaningfully embed learning about different racial and cultural identities within other parts of the setting?
- How is Nathan helping the children to reflect on and understand different cultures?
- How could you apply these principles within your setting?
- This case study can be broken down into several distinct sections: child-initiated play, working with parents, the shopping trip, preparing and eating the food, and refining the learning environment. What do you think Josh and the other children in the setting learnt at each stage of this example?

Throughout this example, Nathan made a series of choices designed to give the children in the setting the freedom to explore their own and different cultures. He created meaningful opportunities for the children to make connections to their own experiences, whilst expanding their horizons and showing that difference is a valuable and enjoyable part of life. The children were encouraged and supported to have respectful conversations about what they liked and did not like, without degrading or dismissing another person's preferences. In doing so, Nathan helped to normalise discussions about the differences and similarities between different racial and cultural identities. By seeking the views of parents and/or carers, Nathan also gave them a voice in the process and built their preferences into the physical environment of the nursery through the display board.

Understanding and respecting difference

Often children will be observed enacting routines that they themselves have experienced, such as feeding, changing nappies, going to work, or putting dolls to bed. This type of play helps children to better understand what their parents do. In this way, pretend play enables children to put themselves in the place of others and to see things from their perspective.

Consider the following examples:

- Four-year-old Carmen is Black. She was observed tying a cloth on her head, tucking in her dolls, and then pretending to go to bed. She told the educator it was her do-rag.[2] This was Carmen's way of exploring and making sense of her mother's bedtime routine.

  In this example, an educator could support Carmen and the other children within the setting by talking about how wrapping your hair at night can help to protect your curls, plaits, or braids. Providing the children with factual and age-appropriate information about differences will help them to understand and respect how Carmen cares for her hair rather than be taken aback by it. For Carmen, these discussions will also serve to validate and normalise her experience.

- Two-year-old Raheem is Muslim and can often be observed in the bathroom playing with running water. One day, an educator noticed Raheem pretending to wash his hands and feet in the sink. Having spoken to Raheem's parents about his faith, the educator realised that this was an important part of his culture that he was enacting – the washing of hands and feet before prayer. It is also a teachable moment. Providing a range of mats, bowls, and jugs in the role play area could help support Raheem as he continues to explore his faith through play.

  In this scenario, educators may also wish to consider how they can widen learning opportunities to all children in the setting, whilst validating Raheem's faith. For example, educators could seek to build different religious festivals and customs into the day-to-day of their practice. In considering how best to do this, it is important to think about how to make these experiences sustained, meaningful, and authentic. That means making it part of children's continuous learning, with opportunities to extend and support learning. Creating one-off, tokenistic activities and then moving on should always be avoided.

As with everything related to race, culture, and religion, it is important that we avoid making generalisations. Just because one child in your setting expresses their faith in one way, does not mean that all children of the same faith will do the same. The extent to which certain religious or cultural practices are observed in families will vary from one family to another. Not all children will have the same religious, racial, or cultural knowledge, even if they identify as being part of a particular religious, racial, or cultural group. That is why it is crucial that educators understand how the children in their setting practice their religion, if they have one, and observe their cultural traditions by working in partnership with the child's parents and/or carers.

Building connections

Educators are also a rich resource that forms an integral part of the physical learning environment of any setting. Sharing aspects of your own racial and cultural identity with the children you work with, their families, and your colleagues can be a wonderful tool to build connections and further enhance the richness of the learning environment. There are many ways to do this, from sharing stories about where you grew up, the food that you love or your favourite traditions to spark discussion, to sharing your reflections and observations with your colleagues to widen the number of perspectives being considered. It is important to remember that this is just as important for White educators to do as it is for educators of colour.

...The School That Tried to End Racism

In 2020, Channel 4 aired the BAFTA-winning documentary series: *The School That Tried to End Racism*. The series follows a secondary school in South London trying to challenge unconscious bias amongst a group of students and, in doing so, shines a spotlight on the impact that racism has on young teenagers. During the experiment, the class is split into two groups – a 'White group' and a 'non-White group' – to discuss their experience of race. When asked if they have ever considered what it means to be White, the White group confessed it was not something they had ever really thought about, with one girl stating: 'It doesn't really mean anything'. In the safety of their group, the non-White students shared a multitude of experiences, dancing, laughing, and singing whilst discussing their racial heritage without fear of judgement.

Having grown up in a White-dominated environment, where Whiteness is presented as the 'norm', it is easy to understand why a White child may never have had to ask themselves what it means to be White. After all, when you see yourself reflected everywhere, you become insulated from the race-based stress that many people of colour experience (DiAngelo, 2019). For the latter, the daily (if not thrice daily) reminders that you are an 'outsider' often lead to greater awareness of your own and others' racial identity.

However, as with all racial groups, White is not a homogeneous racial category. There are many similarities and differences that can and should be explored, including a multitude of traditions, languages, and cultural practices. The absence of reflection and understanding about what it means to be White can have a profoundly negative effect on White children who are likely to grow up unaware of the systemic inequalities caused by racial discrimination and prejudice as a result. As Derman-Sparks and Ramsey argue, 'White children first need to explore and respect the range of differences and similarities among white people...To heighten children's awareness of differences in relatively homogeneous classrooms, we suggest exploring the diversity that *is* the classroom' (n.d.: 4).[3] Educators are an important part of that classroom and the stories you share can teach the children in your settings important lessons about belonging, proactively countering any view that difference equates to inferiority.

The very act of seeing educators open up and share their own experiences helps to foster mutual respect and understanding and supports a two-way exchange. After completing the Froebel Trust's Element 6 training course, which is focused on equality, equity, diversity, and inclusion, the staff at Sycamore Nursery (*name has been changed*) committed to sharing more about themselves and learning more about one another. One of the first things they decided to change was their staff notice board; rather than just including pictures and names, they expanded the notice board to include further information, such as where each member of staff is from, what languages they speak, and what their pronouns are.

Upon seeing how successful this change was at opening up a dialogue, the staff extended this approach to the children in their settings and their families by encouraging them to share information about themselves, including photos which reflect their life outside of nursery. This information was compiled into a photo album that everyone could access, including other parents, so that the children's learning could continue at home. Parents and guardians are now also asked to complete 'all about me' forms before their children start with the nursery. These forms have been designed using inclusive language such as 'parent/guardian one' and 'parent/guardian two' rather than 'mother' and 'father' and ask what languages they speak. It also provides space for parents and/or carers to share any other information that they think might be helpful or relevant, giving families the space to share anything that is important to them or their children. Using this information, the staff at Sycamore Nursery described feeling better able to build connections and identify teachable moments, drawing on their own experiences to further learning.

Knowing how and when to intervene

Children's attitudes towards difference and their disposition for learning can be heavily influenced by the feedback they receive from educators, and the feedback they observe us giving others, including non-verbal communication. Our approach to teaching and the physical content of our educational settings needs to be robust enough to promote culturally sensitive, informative, and age-appropriate exploration of different cultures if we are to successfully provide strong counter-narratives to the prejudice and stereotypes children may have absorbed elsewhere. You can do this by:

- Responding genuinely to young children's interests;
- Using every encounter with children as an opportunity to connect with them;
- Recognising and respecting difference; and

- Proactively challenging and countering stereotypes and assumptions by facilitating positive discussions about people of different races, ethnicities, religions, and cultures.

Case study – making tea

Jasmine and Alisha, both aged three years and six months, were pretending to make tea in the home corner outside all morning. Jasmine is White and Alisha is South Asian, with parents of Bangladeshi descent. The girls had been happily preparing food together until Alisha put a pot on the stove and poured water into it, stating: 'I'm going to make some tea'. Jasmine looked confused. 'No', she said, 'that's not how you do it' and proceeded to act out filling the kettle with water.

'No', said Alisha, 'this is how my grandma makes tea'. Alisha put a selection of stones, conkers, sticks, and shells into the pot, telling Jasmine that they were the herbs and spices needed to make tea, continuously stirring throughout.

Whilst Alisha was stirring, Jasmine became progressively more irritated by the way Alisha was making tea. 'Look', Jasmine snapped, 'this is how you do it', and pretended to put a teabag into her mug. Jasmine then poured the water from the kettle into her mug, adding milk and sugar. She left her mug on the table and told Alisha that she was letting her tea brew.

Alisha started to look around the home corner for something. She couldn't find what she was looking for, so she went over to the sand tray, returning with a small sieve. She used this to strain the herbs and spices out of her tea. Both girls sat down at different tables, ignoring each other, pretending to drink their tea.

The educator observing this interaction later overheard the girls arguing about how tea is made and continued to leave them to sort it out themselves. The two girls refused to play together for the rest of the day.

In this case, both girls came into the home corner knowing something about their culture, and the reality is that both were right. However, rather than ending their play having learnt something about the multitude of ways people make tea and, in turn, learning something valuable about another child's culture, they both left unable to fully appreciate the value of the experience that the other child brought.

The play scenario that the girls were involved in naturally created opportunities for them to learn about each other, but they needed to be guided by an educator that understood how their home cultures influenced their play. In this example, the educator could have chosen to talk to the children about the differences and similarities in the way they made tea and encouraged empathy. Questions such as 'How did it make you feel when Jasmine made tea differently to you?', 'How do you think Alisha felt when you said she was making tea incorrectly?', or 'Did you know there are many ways to make tea? Would you like to learn how Alisha (or Jasmine) makes it?' could have helped to bridge the divide. This would have helped both girls to understand their different behaviours as well as deepen their understanding and respect for each other.

The diversity of cultural experiences

Because stereotyping and prejudice begin to form in early childhood, it is important that a diversity of cultural experiences is represented within the physical learning environment to enhance understanding and minimise bias. Learning about different cultural practices in meaningful ways can help children to engage with and appreciate differences between cultures, as opposed to seeing differences as a problem. These connections matter, and it is part of an educator's role to provide the framework within which these connections are made.

Case study – making challah

A table had been set up with a baking activity to make challah.[4] The children were experimenting with strings of dough, making different shapes. Three-year-old Alice came over and wanted a turn. She helped to prepare three strands of dough, and, with minimal support, she crisscrossed the dough to make the traditional challah shape. 'I do this at home with my mummy', she said proudly.

In the same setting, just a few months apart, two-year-old Mai was observed with a large stick, tapping it, and banging it around the room very close to other children. The educators were very concerned about his behaviour. They thought it was disruptive, a bit violent, and asked Mai to stop – that is, until they spoke to his mother. She informed them that in the Maori culture, when a new building is opened, there is a ceremony involving sticks. Mai had been to several such ceremonies and was re-enacting them to make sense of his experience. The educators did not initially understand what Mai was doing was linked culturally to his understanding of his experiences as his behaviour was at odds with their expectations of acceptable behaviour.

Without speaking to Mai's parents and building an awareness of Mai's culture, the educators in his setting could have left Mai with a lasting inner conflict – one that told him his culture was wrong and disruptive, creating feelings of confusion and shame – whilst supporting Alice to see the beauty and value in hers. Whilst this disparity in support may have been an unwitting mistake on the part of the educators in this setting, the impact had the potential to be no less damaging. It could have significantly dented Mai's confidence, ultimately teaching him that his Maori traditions were not acceptable outside of his home.

Regardless of our intentions, our words and our behaviours have an impact. Nobody expects you to know it all but, as educators, we owe it to the children we teach to learn from them, their families, and the world around us, and to reflect, reassess, and pivot when we get it wrong. This means learning about the cultural practices, customs, and traditions that are familiar to the children we teach in their everyday lives so we can provide opportunities for them to connect to and make sense of their experiences. It also involves carving out time for regular reflection, so that we can challenge our own bias and consider whether the behaviours that we may frown upon may be culturally influenced in some way.

Celebrating diversity and reducing inequality in the learning environment

Creating a rich learning environment in which all children can engage in a diversity of experiences will take time to establish and should be a continuous process. No matter how good it is, developing an activity about race that takes place one day a year or buying one Black doll (as Laura discusses in the Foreword of this book) is *not* and will *never* be enough. We need to move beyond tokenism and embrace regular and meaningful ways to build a culture of diversity and inclusion within the physicality of our settings.

Before coming to nursery, children will have their own experiences of diversity. Educators will need to help them connect with and understand other children despite differences. It takes skill to create a learning environment in which children can explore and discover, and where educators focus on supporting children's social and creative development. As part of their personal, social, and emotional development, educators must help support every child to understand issues of fairness and equity because doing so increases children's ability to empathise and exposes them to more respectful and appropriate ways to respond to difference.

There are many things that educators can do to provide meaningful opportunities for learning:

- Providing children with opportunities to create and display self-portraits is one way you can celebrate difference and foster a positive sense of identity. When children are given the opportunity to talk about themselves and their home culture in the school or setting, this can lead to them feeling a sense of pride in who they are, as well as giving others an insight into their everyday life. Children will benefit from opportunities to talk about themselves at carpet or circle time, including through activities that encourage them to bring in objects from home to talk about and share with their peers. Educators can use these opportunities to counter and challenge assumptions that children may have about others and support them in developing the skills that they need to respect others.
- As shown through the case study about Josh's chicken, you can encourage children to talk about the different types of food that they have at home. You can ask parents to make a dish that all children can try or get children to make simple dishes and talk to them about food from different places. Another option could be supporting children to write their own cookbook of their favourite dishes. To extend their learning, you can use these activities as an opportunity to make meaningful links to the ecology, climate, and culture of the countries that the dishes originated from. Think big: a simple cooking activity can support children to cover all areas of the curriculum.

- Exposing children to music and musical instruments from around the world, not just European ones, is vital. Why not talk to children about the types of music they like to dance, sing, or listen to and how it makes them feel? You could ask children to draw or dance while listening to different types of music and observe their individual expressions. (See Chapter 6 for more ideas on how to extend children's understanding of different races, ethnicities, and cultures through music).

- Language helps children feel connected. Consider how you can expose children to different languages and provide opportunities for children to see and hear the language they speak at home represented in the environment. Be careful not to focus on a child's inability to speak English. Instead, celebrate what they can do. Focusing too much on what children cannot do may narrow the learning opportunities available and could lead you to lower your expectations of them. Children are sensitive to the feedback of educators and when this happens, it can cause children to feel that the language they speak at home is not valued, or that they are not as 'good' as those with English as a first language.

Working with families

The final element to consider when designing a setting is how you work with families. Parental involvement is a key feature of creating an effective physical learning environment, since it brings together personal knowledge and professional knowledge about the child (Whalley, 2001). When educators base their judgements on assumptions rather than the personal knowledge that parents and/or carers have about their child, then power struggles may emerge, and the results are often weighted heavily in favour of the educator. Without giving due consideration to how a child's cultural, racial, and/or religious identity plays out at home, educators may find that they are consciously or unconsciously telling some children and their families that they do not belong.

Educators may find home visits a useful tool to get to know children and their families well, but they should be approached sensitively, recognising that not all families will automatically welcome them. Care should be taken to avoid intrusive questions that could alienate and/or offend.

Reflective questions

- How do you provide space for parents and carers to share ideas of what they would like to see?
- Could you speak to parents, carers, or local community groups about donating culturally relevant items from their homes, such as empty spice bottles or hair and skincare products?
- Could you go further than this and borrow items of cultural significance from parents, carers, or local community groups, such as a yarmulke (a skullcap often worn by Jewish men) or a traditional cheongsam (a Chinese dress worn by women), to spark discussions and provide a valuable learning moment? How can you extend these learning opportunities through other activities to avoid tokenism?

Educators should be consistently welcoming and approachable to children and their families. To do this successfully, you should consider both the emotional learning environment (discussed in Chapter 3) and the physical environment; the two should weave together to create truly safe spaces for open and collaborative discussions that enhance children's emotional wellbeing and create a sense of belonging. This is a key tenet of anti-racist pedagogy, rooted in developing respectful relationships with children and their families. According to the Department for Children, Schools and Families (2009), educators are better able to assist each child's learning journey if they are familiar with the children and families. When this is done, children are recognised as being both an individual and a member of different groups (e.g., a family, a cultural community, etc.), allowing their unique needs to shine through. This enables diversity to not only be recognised but embraced.

Transforming the learning environment

Through their exploration of a well-structured learning environment, children will learn a range of skills with appropriate adult guidance. The learning environment must therefore seek to support children's development, both indoors and outdoors. As this chapter has shown, the learning experiences on offer should be culturally relevant and specific to the children's home culture and their first-hand experiences. Understanding and responding to the needs of children that we work with is fundamental to providing a high-quality learning environment. Consideration also needs to be given to how schools or settings show understanding of the different races, cultures, and faiths represented in the local community.

To transform the learning environment, we have to be open and honest about the differences that children and families bring to the school or setting. When these factors are not acknowledged or valued, discrimination is likely to persist. As educators, we should strive to make sure that different races and cultures are represented in our settings and, if they are not, it is our responsibility to escalate any gaps we identify and push for more inclusive resources. After all, what is not seen in the learning environment, is just as important as what is.

Notes

1 Fufu is a popular West African dish which is often made of cassava dough – a starchy root vegetable similar to sweet potatoes or yams. It should be eaten with your hands and is a side dish used to scoop up soup or stew.
2 A do-rag is a cloth that is tied around the top of your head to protect your hair. It is often used by people of Afro-Caribbean descent at night.
3 Derman-Sparks and Ramsey define the 'dominant norm' as 'a family with two, heterosexual parents, middle or upper class, Christian, urban or suburban, private home, able-bodied' (n.d.:4).
4 Challah is a type of bread eaten in a Jewish home on the Sabbath/Friday night.

References

Bruce, T. (1987) *Early Childhood Education*. London. Hodder and Stoughton.
Cadwell, L. (1997) *Bringing Reggio Emilia Home: An Innovative Approach to Early Childhood Education*. New York: Teachers College Press.
Coard, B. (2021) *How the West Indian Child is Made Educationally Sub-Normal in the British School System*. Expanded 5th edn. Kingston: McDermott Publishing.
Commonwealth Immigrants Advisory Council (1964) *Second Report by the Commonwealth Immigrants Advisory Council*. Cmnd 2266. London: HMSO, February.

Department for Children, Schools and Families (2009) *The National Strategies: Early Years. Building Futures: Believing in Children.* London: Department for Children, Schools and Families.

Department for Education and Skills (2007) *Diversity and Citizenship Curriculum Review. (The Ajegbo Report).* London: Department for Education and Skills.

Derman-Sparks, L. and Ramsey, P. (n.d.) *"What if All the Kids are White?" Multicultural / Anti-Bias Education with White Children.* Available at: https://www.teachingforchange.org/wp-content/uploads/2012/08/ec_whatifallthekids_english.pdf.

DiAngelo, R. (2019) *White Fragility.* London: Penguin Books.

Froebel Trust (2023) *Short Courses: Developing Knowledgeable and Nurturing Educators.* London: Froebel Trust. Available at: https://www.froebel.org.uk/uploads/documents/FT_Short_Courses_brochure.pdf

Froebel, F. (1887) *The Education of Man.* New York: Appleton.

Grosvenor, I. (1997) *Assimilating Identities: Racism and Educational Policy in Post 1945 Britain.* London: Lawrence and Wishart.

Manning-Morton, J. (2004) 'Birth to Three, Your Guide to Developing Quality Provision'. *Nursery World Magazine,* 17 June, pp.18–19.

McGeary, X. (2021) 'How to Make Your Setting Culturally Inclusive'. *Famly,* 21 April. Available at: https://www.famly.co/blog/making-your-early-years-setting-culturally-inclusive.

Montessori, M. (2016) *The Absorbent Mind.* Amsterdam: Montessori-Pierson Publishing Company.

Shain, F. (2013) 'Race, Nation and Education: An Overview of British Attempts to 'Manage Diversity' Since the 1950s'. *Education Inquiry,* 4(1), pp.63–85.

The School That Tried to End Racism (2020) 'Channel 4, 25 June and 2 July'. Available at: https://www.channel4.com/programmes/the-school-that-tried-to-end-racism

Whalley, M. and The Pen Green Team (2001) *Involving parents in their Children's Learning.* London: Paul Chapman.

6

The truth about the music we teach

Professor Nathan Holder

The music used in early years settings finds itself in a unique position. Around the world, parents and educators know that music forms an integral part of a child's formative years – supporting cognitive development, auditory perception, motor skills, and expanding their vocabulary – yet there is not only a distinct lack of music specialists in the early years, but amongst those who do teach, a lack of confidence is also commonly cited (Welch, 2021). One of the reasons for this lack of confidence is the 'misconception that musicality is defined by success in Western Art music' (Welch, 2021). This is not only an issue in early years music education (hereafter EYME) – it also appears throughout formal education as parents, carers, and educators figure out ways to teach and learn about music, with an understanding that academic success usually takes the form of degrees and certificates.

Due to the composition of the workforce in the UK, young children are likely to only interact with White women during their time in early years education (Department for Education, 2021). Potential educators of colour, who have minimal experience working with the music of Western Europe originating from the 16th–19th centuries, but have a passion for early years education, may shy away from becoming music educators (Welch, 2021). This results in the music that is offered to children in educational settings often being constructed within the boundaries of Whiteness with little input from Black, Brown, and Indigenous peoples. Limited repertoire and representation therefore become major issues, and the opportunity to provide gateways for children to construct their racial identities gets lost.[1]

If we recognise that music is an integral part of life, how can we help children to not only experience a variety of music, but to do so in an authentic way that helps them to understand themselves and the world around them?

DOI: 10.4324/9781003251149-8

Is music neutral?

Much of the music aimed at children is often presented as neutral and harmless, when in fact the opposite may be true. One of the general effects of colonialism on music education has been to predominantly use music which makes little reference to specific cultures or peoples and to teach children using music using Western European ideas of melody and harmony. Looking at the world through a postcolonial lens, we can see how Whiteness dominates ideas around not only how music is taught, but who gets to teach it, and who is represented within it. These pedagogical ideas have been systematically imposed by a dominant White culture, which has asserted itself through colonial exploitation, racism, and oppressive behaviours. The result is an early years musical framework created in the image of White Europeanness which manifests in a variety of different ways, and necessarily perpetuates itself as a means to continually assert musical, intellectual, and moral superiority. Without sustained input, critique, and creation from people of colour, this mechanism will continue to give children a narrow view and understanding of what music is in education settings.

The roots of these practices were conceived during the Enlightenment, which 'introduced the idea that behaviour and attitudes can be modified through the formal acquisition of knowledge and understanding' (Drummond, 2008). In this way, the danger is that music education becomes about helping children to think and see the world in specific ways, rather than encouraging a wide range of experiences even at an early age. For example, the song 'The Wheels on the Bus' has many limitations in teaching children about what a bus is and how it might function. Around the world, buses can be referred to as ZRs, maxis, or matatus, and by learning to only refer to it as a bus, this is a small way in which children begin to separate what is 'normal' from 'other'.

This is especially true for children of colour whose parents' or carers' experiences are firmly rooted in cultures from the Global South; what they learn at home and in education settings can be extremely different.[2]

As this dominant culture spread its ideologies in systematically violent ways, particularly throughout the 17th–19th centuries, traditions emerged which became globalised and codified themselves in language, politics, and music. As formal music education formed in the Global North, it has done so with a singular frame of reference and understanding about what music is, what it can be used for, and how it is to be perceived and taught.[3] Unchallenged, these ideas present themselves as neutral and served the dominant culture as its default epistemology, until mass migration, and post-colonial theories revealed that these epistemologies were not universal. For example, 'orchestra' is defined by the Cambridge dictionary as, 'a large group of musicians who play many different instruments together and are led by a conductor'. The now default assumption that an orchestra means an ensemble as constructed in Western Europe in the 19th century erases long traditions of ensembles in various continents who play music outside of the Western classical tradition.

When thinking about music and neutrality, there are a few things to consider in the construction of activities for the children in your setting.

Lyrics

Lyrics in any language or dialect give us insight into not only who may have written a song, but who a song may be intended for. In addition to this, there may be geographical, cultural, and/or generational signifiers which can be easily identified by some and/or alienate others. Before choosing a song, you may wish to consider the following questions:

- What language is the song in?
- Who wrote the song?
- Have any racist/sexist/homophobic lyrics been changed?
- Do the lyrics give any clues about a particular place or culture?
- What is this song teaching?
- Can you give context for parents and/or carers about the song to further extend a child's learning at home?

Instrumentation

Instruments can reveal where or even when music was created. While music from different geographical locations may be sung or listened to, by being played on a guitar or piano for example, it can change the meaning of the song. It also speaks to the commodification and appropriation of music if/when this occurs. For example, a traditional Japanese folk song played on a violin, or a folk song from Uganda played on a recorder may reveal the impact of colonialism, and attitudes rooted in White supremacy or appropriation. Consider:

- Which instruments can you hear?
- Across all of your repertoire, can you hear the same instruments?
- If there is a video, who are playing the instruments?

Rhythms

Many styles of music utilise unique rhythms which help to differentiate one style from another. For example, reggae uses rhythms which differentiate it from samba, soca, or the blues. Reggae evolved in Jamaica, and its development along with some of its most famous exponents, are inextricably tied to the sociopolitical struggles of the 1960s, 1970s, and 1980s. The same is true for other styles of music – their rhythms are linked to their places of origin, peoples, and sociopolitical struggles. Ask yourself:

- Across the repertoire, is there much variation in rhythm?
- Do these rhythms come from a variety of places and times?
- Is dance encouraged? Is the dancing modelled authentic?

Singing/vocal styles

In the UK, it can be common to hear singers who have a London accent, and less common to hear accents from the southwest, or north of England for example. Also, we find that certain pitch ranges and levels of vibrato are more common than others. A singer or speaker who accentuates certain words due to dialect, familiarity with language of choice, give indications as to who is singing, and who they are singing to. The differences between the sound quality of a person's voice can also inform children of any age, regardless of the level of lyrical comprehension. Ask yourself the following questions:

- Is there a range of low- and high-pitched voices?
- Can you hear a range of different dialects and accents?

The above is not to say that one must intentionally seek out or attempt to create music for the sake of it. All music has meaning, and children and adults make assumptions and form ideas based on the cues that they hear. If the majority of music interacted with is, for example, English folk songs sung by a White woman playing a guitar, there are clear messages implied – are people of colour 'permitted' to sing to children? How about men, trans, and non-binary folx? What music is valued by society and what is not? If there is no 'neutral' music, it therefore becomes important to consider the covert messages being transmitted and ensure that children are exposed to a balance which may be codified in any of the above. All music contains messages, subtle or otherwise, which are to be understood when considering the musical offering of any setting.

Reflective questions

- How much music in your setting is from a culture outside of Western Europe?
- How much music in your setting was created by a person of colour?
- Do you select songs with lyrics in a variety of different languages?

Bridging gaps

As discussed earlier in this chapter, White women make up the majority of the early years workforce in the UK (Department for Education, 2021). The impact that this particular demographic makeup of the workforce has on the lens through which children are taught is not considered as much as it should be. Even with the best of intentions, the music in many EYME settings can lean towards an approach which excludes the music and experiences of Black and Brown folx. Children can find themselves stuck between the music they listen, dance to, and hear at home, and the music they learn about in educational settings – this creates a division between what is 'acceptable' at home and at school and teaches children to hide part of themselves in different settings to fit the dominant culture (also known as 'code-switching'). While this undoubtedly affects everyone, it is children of colour who suffer the most, with those existing at the intersections of gender and disability and other protected characteristics facing additional barriers.

To try and understand the different musical experiences a child might have, here are four categories to consider how to bridge the musical gaps between EYME settings and at home.

Familiar music

This describes music which is frequently listened to and interacted with, including music attached to various religions, culturally significant and popular tunes or melodies. Associations are quickly made by young children between dance moves and particular words, styles, or melodies, whether they be through recorded mediums (such as video) played on instruments or sung. There is a clear association with particular music and people or places, which may cause surprise when heard outside of familiar contexts. It is often this music which forms the basis of childhood musical experiences, learned either through a musical environment or regular teaching with an understanding of its performative nature. For example, this may occur in a church setting, where children are exposed to a repertoire of songs which they may hear or see as part of a performance (or act of worship), learned with others in similar age brackets, and reinforced in a home setting.

Conscious music

This describes music which is frequently listened to and interacted with, but rarely formally reinforced. While this music may have little cultural significance, it may form part of a temporary social culture in the form of TV or radio adverts, which may permeate into consciousness for a limited period of time. It may even be a song which is extremely popular for a period of time.

Peripheral music

This is music that may be heard, but rarely interacted with. These include adverts, theme tunes, or songs heard in everyday life. They are not reinforced by anyone but may be slightly recognisable. As cognitive ability and language skills develop, this type of music may be vaguely familiar to children, or form part of a nostalgic experience within a niche social group.

School music

This type of music is created purely for educational purposes and often sits outside of the other categories unless it is reinforced in education or socially. When educational music, influenced by the myth of neutrality, fails to understand, or include cultural signifiers or references, it remains separate from social and cultural life and exists in a bubble. Given that early years education marks the beginning of a journey of self-discovery for children, particularly for those whose sociocultural identities are in a content state of flux (for various reasons, including sociopolitical and personal/familial reasons), this becomes a lost opportunity for learning.

Reflective questions

- Are you aware of music that falls into each of these categories for children in your setting?
- Do you understand the significance of each type of music?
- Does some of this music overlap with your own experiences?
- Is some of this music included in your practice? Should it be? Could it be?
- After reading this, can you identify any gaps in the music used in your setting?
- How could you rectify the gaps you have identified?

To try and address these gaps, repertoire and pedagogy should be considered to ensure that the musical offering in the early years is able to relate to the various ways children interact with and process music.

Repertoire

Songs such as *Kye Kye Kule* have been repeated and taught in many early years settings, without much inquiry as to their origins, language, appropriateness, or the validity of associated actions. The vast majority of inquiry into these aspects of songs often comes from second- or third-hand accounts – specifically in the case of *Kye Kye Kule*, blog posts suggesting that conversations with an often unnamed Ghanaian man have resulted in it being used as a version of *Head, Shoulders, Knees, and Toes.*

Kye Kye Kule

Kye kye kule ×2
Kye kye kofi nsa ×2
Kofi nsa langa ×2
Kaka shi langa ×2
Kum adende ×2
Kum adende Hey!

Where there is such ambiguity over the origin and meaning of a song, alternatives can be found which are not only culturally accurate and pedagogically sound but have been created by the very people who come from Ghana, Indonesia, or China for example. A song such as *Me Ti M'Abati,* which is in Twi (a dialect of the Akan language most commonly spoken in Ghana) and is translated as *Heads, Shoulders, Knees, and Toes,* can be used.

Me Ti M'Abati

Me Ti (head)
M'abati (shoulders)
Me Kotodwe (knees)
Me Nansoaa (toes) ×3
Ne nyianaa ka me nipaduaho (This is my whole body)

There are, of course, a myriad of songs to sing from and about various different cultures, which can be found very easily. *Me Ti M'Abati* is an example of a song which explores different parts of the body in Twi and by taking a similar approach, one can find songs in different languages which perform the same function. Counting up to five in different languages such as Spanish, Igbo, and Urdu is another easy link to make, which may create an environment of acceptance for children who speak English as a second language. Singing in different languages also forms a fundamental and early role in children's understandings of society, helping them to form links between the people they may interact with in the classroom, and in wider society. It is the beginning of interacting with various cultures at this early stage of development which can help to form positive attitudes towards others who look and sound different to themselves. It is a shift away from ensuring that all children are able to learn a limited selection of specific songs in specific ways, and exposing children to many different styles, people, and languages which can help to set the foundations of culturally aware and culturally respectful children.

A great way to introduce more cultural diversity into a setting is to find versions or lyrics of songs in different languages. Many songs made for children are sung around the world, in different languages or with different words which make them more culturally relevant. Children, parents, and/or carers themselves will often have an incredible repertoire of music that is listened to at home or in social settings – songs which work for them and which can be shared very easily. This not only helps the repertoire to be relevant to children in a setting but can also help parents feel more included in their children's learning and develop a closer relationship with teachers after feeling seen and respected.

Reflective questions

- Are there any children in your setting who are used to speaking or listening to different languages at home?
- Could parents and/or carers of the children in your care share familiar songs such as *Heads, Shoulders, Knees, and Toes* in their languages?
- Can you find recordings of songs in languages children may understand to play in your setting?
- Are you aware of the origins of the songs you sing or listen to?
- Have you taught or played a song while assuming the nationalities and ethnicities of the children in the room?

Songs with racist pasts

Unfortunately, there are many songs in circulation which attempt to depict a certain culture but have instead caused great offence to specific communities. It is important that children are not exposed to music which might be harmful to them and their parents and/or carers. One of the great things about music is its memorability – attaching a tune to a piece of information is a quick way to make that information memorable. Tunes which are either harmful or inauthentic can become easily internalised and leave children with questions when they grow up and realise what they have been singing or playing. There are many music educators worldwide who are only now realising that the music they have been teaching or playing for 20-plus years has been rooted in racism.

Often, these songs work for those who regurgitate the lessons and repertoire of their teachers or professors without critical inquiry as to the where's, why's, and cultural relevance of a song or tune. This is not to say that there is a wholesale and deliberate willingness not to interrogate repertoire or pedagogy, but rarely does critical inquiry extend to ideas of culture outside of one's own, especially if one is situated in a society in which repertoires from Black, Brown, or Indigenous cultures are experienced as 'exotic', 'cool', or 'fun'.

The idea that songs such as *Land of the Silver Birch* or *Five Little Monkeys* cannot be considered racist if there is no explicitly derogatory language is a fallacy. While songs using racial slurs have all but been eliminated (and not without resistance), the origins of many of these songs are anything but innocent. While the lyrics to certain songs have been changed over the years to become more politically correct, the evidence of their racist histories or indeed the racist attitudes of the people who composed them, have either been recently discovered or ignored. It should never have been acceptable to sing *Pick a Bale of Cotton* and encourage children to act it out, but this occurred because some White educators ignored the voices of Black educators, parents, and history, believing that no harm was being caused in the singing of such songs due to the belief that we are now living in a post-racial society. As White people make up the vast majority of music educators and policymakers in the early years, there is a responsibility incumbent on all White educators and policy advisors to investigate, reflect, and ensure the safeguarding of all children through their music provision.

Where the canon of non-English music in early years from Black, Brown, or Indigenous communities remains minuscule, the songs which exist within the current canon constitute the full diversity of song choices and are therefore protected as one would an endangered species. The removal or recontextualisation of one or a few well-known songs threatens to unbalance the carefully constructed musical ecosystem in which the music of Black and Brown and Indigenous people exist in the shadows, integral to the system for the purposes of upholding the virtue signalling status quo. As the educator Martin Urbach writes, 'How fitting of White supremacy culture that White teachers perceive that once we get rid [of] the racist songs, there won't be any songs left to sing' (Urbach, 2019).

It can be challenging to replace a song which has a racist past, especially one which may be so embedded into early years repertoire, precisely because this is often how Whiteness manifests itself. Educators and publishers can be hesitant to revisit and refresh repertoire, often citing that these songs are pedagogically sound as they have not received any complaints before. Questioning, 'Who do these songs work for?' and, 'Why were there no complaints?' can reveal not only the failings of a homogenous workforce and resistance to change, but the power dynamics at play in a society in which Whiteness is default.

By including people from marginalised cultures in consulting on repertoire and curricula, many mistakes can be easily avoided. Especially in racially homogeneous spaces, the voices of the oppressed need to be centred when any ambiguity around their culture surfaces. The more the voices of the oppressed are centred, the process towards an equitable and culturally responsive early years music education can accelerate. Without equal collaboration from those of marginalised cultures, efforts made towards this 'would be a contradiction in terms if the oppressors not only defended but actually implemented a liberating education' (Friere, 1970).

Some of these ideas are rooted in decolonial theory and express a desire to improve outcomes for communities who statistically underperform in education consistently, and who often belong to the most marginalised groups. Black Caribbean, Roma, and Bangladeshi groups in England are constantly behind their White peers and culturally relevant pedagogy seeks to address this by helping students to develop, understand, and 'affirm their own cultural identity while developing critical perspectives that challenge inequities that schools (and other institutions) perpetuate' (Ladson-Billings, 1995). It is no coincidence that this style of pedagogy was devised by a Black woman, as Black women have often had to navigate the intersection between sex and race, contributing intellectually to pedagogy and critical thought, while fighting against stereotypical 'mammy' archetypes and largely excluded from representation within music education. As the foundation of education, early years is the perfect place to attempt to dismantle the structures which continue to impact the most marginalised groups. It is important to critically examine all songs in the repertoire at regular intervals in order to ensure that the music is meeting the needs of every child in your setting.

The importance of visual representation

In providing music for children, appropriate visuals for children can be key to their understanding the world and their place in it. Especially in music from Black, Brown, or Indigenous communities, there is a startling lack of accurate visual representation in music education. The inaccurate representation and misrepresentation of cultures occur when a dominant culture chooses what and how to represent the culture of marginalised groups without consent or consideration. Dixon (1977), for example, identifies ways in which subtle and overt racist attitudes find their way into children's literature. While this chapter focuses on music, it is not difficult to see how similar rules apply. Dixon states that where young children's literature may rely on pictures rather than text to tell a story, symbolic representation at that age can reinforce racist attitudes without explicit terms and offensive language. If we follow this logic, this means that in music education, the visual representations which accompany any music also need to be paid attention to. There have been many harmful, if not strange, representations of cultures including *Pappadum* by The Wiggles, who repeat the word 'poppadom' while wearing *shalwar kameez*, saris, and brandishing cricket bats. There are many creators of colour who are making videos, posters, and music which authentically represent themselves, which should be used instead. In understanding how visual representation can enhance musical learning, it is important to be aware of the visual imagery young children are being presented with.

Ideally, the music which children interact with should be (but not be limited to) these things:

- **Musical** – that which affirms and expands children's knowledge and experience of various elements of music, including tempo, rhythm, and pitch.

- **Culturally relevant** – being an accurate representation of a culture(s) or groups, helping children to find and celebrate their own identities through music.
- **Diverse** – music created by a range of people, in different styles, places, and times.
- **Inclusive** – all children are able to take part to the best of their individual capabilities.
- **Fun** – engaging and enjoyable.

Representation in music

Whilst representation of Black, Brown, and Indigenous people in early years music may be scarce, representation for representation's sake is not the answer. As children develop an increased sense of self, the accurate and symbolic representation of people becomes increasingly important. In recent years, Disney has removed movies such as *Dumbo* and *Peter Pan* from its streaming site Disney+ due to the representation and depiction of Jim Crow and Indigenous Americans respectively. There is widespread acknowledgement that these images are harmful and perpetuate the racist views of the time, which have left millions of children with disturbing views about groups they may never have interacted with. (See Chapter 4 for more of a discussion on race and representation.)

In striving towards a music education which accurately represents people, places, and cultures, care must be taken when images are being selected to pair with music which may speak to culture(s) of students in the classroom. If no music can be absolutely neutral, the same can be said for images, each of which reveals things about the subject. Solely portraying music from the African continent with images of mud huts and traditional dresses not only gives a partial image of the continent, but one of poverty and exoticism, aligned with many images from mainstream media. A music education devoid of the intention to expose children to an equitable representation of people, their identities, society, and how they 'musick' (Small, 1998) perpetuates Whiteness and halts efforts which seek to bring about equity and justice to marginalised groups.

Music sessions can provide an excellent opportunity for young children to see people who they can relate to and aspire to be like. The ability through resources – such as YouTube, TikTok, and Instagram – to show children the faces and places behind the music, music makers, and others who have influenced culture in various ways is changing how we teach and learn. It all starts with an educator understanding how their positionality will impact not only the selection of music played and interacted with, but also how different forms of music, people, and cultures are represented. Without constant inquiry into who we are, what we like, and what we believe to be good, a musical offering may only speak to the educator's own power and bias. This will, in various ways, affect all children in a setting. Some may feel as though the musical environment in their educational setting is an extension of their home environment, which may result in them becoming deeply embedded in their own music and culturally unaware of music outside of these spaces. Other children may feel alienated, only gaining an understanding of their teacher's way of experiencing music and clearly distinguish between music in a home environment and an educational setting as being very different. The dissonance between these two spaces helps to create the beginning of the attainment gaps between children of different cultures and ethnicities, which can be observed throughout the early years and widen as children progress through formal education. Without intentionally thinking about the needs of the most marginalised groups, the same problems will continue to be perpetuated. This becomes more important if the children in any given setting are not provided with opportunities to create and make music that is meaningful to them. If only the teacher serves as the expert, this sends powerful messages to children about what is expressed, played, and valued.

It is important to consider the bias that exists within music and begin a reflective and reflexive journey towards ensuring that a musical offering includes and represents all in attendance.

Reflective questions

Consider the following:

- How have your personal tastes influenced the music which you teach and/or play for children?
- How much music have you learned from the children/parents/carers you interact with?
- How do you represent music from around the world in a meaningful way, and how often do you do this?

Appropriate music

Typically, the music offered to children in the early years tends to be specifically created with an ear toward simplicity. There is an implicit assumption that music offered to children needs to be sufficiently simple, with monosyllabic words or short phrases which need to be recognisable. Where have these ideas come from?

In their home environment, many children will listen to the music played by older siblings, parents, and/or carers, and increasingly use YouTube and TikTok, which will expose them to an increasing array of music. Even music contained in adverts, while not meant for children, can become some of the most familiar music to them, given the frequency at which they appear. Outside of songs which talk explicitly about sex, violence, and drugs, there are many songs and styles which can expand a child's horizons beyond songs about fruit and animals. The fact is that many children can create made-up syllables or dances in time to the music or rhythms that they hear. These lyrics may be in different languages or consist of scales other than major or minor ones.

Classical music is often thought of as a style which is universal in its appeal, contains no profanity, and provides the added benefits of increasing IQ, even for a limited time (Rauscher, 1993). However, the belief that classical music is neutral and best for learning is rooted in White supremacy. It forms the basis of music education in the Global North and many other places around the world due to colonialism and imperialism, with children being encouraged to listen to it at the very beginning of their musical journeys, in the hope that it will constitute a firm foundation upon which to build musically from. With this forming the foundation of pedagogy, styles such as hip hop, Afrobeat, reggae, soca, and other contemporary styles produced by people of the Global South are often dismissed as 'inappropriate'. Often, the dismissal of whole styles of music occurs due to mainstream media depictions and the absence of those styles from an educator's own listening habits. Hip hop, in particular, suffers from this, even though there is a lot of hip hop that children can benefit from (Holder, 2020). It is Whiteness armed with the history and ideology of classical music which allows for the music of the self-proclaimed pederast Camille Saint-Saëns to be played for children across the world, while demonising Black and Brown musicians for their depictions of fictitious violence. The fact is, hip hop pedagogy can provide children with the opportunity to engage with rhythm, pitch, and texture while contributing to phonetic development. Coupled with the fact that many children will be familiar with vocal cadences and localised styles such as trap or grime, the failure to include elements of hip hop represents an unwillingness to listen to and seek out music and lyrics free from violence, misogyny, or drug references.

It is also important to remember that music does not need to be taught within traditional ideas of what a music lesson for young children should look like. In trying to prepare children for life in our diverse and ever-changing world, 'students must understand their own historical and cultural heritage and those of others within their communities and beyond' (Consortium of National Arts Education Associations, 1994: 26). If children are exposed to a range of music, the question must be asked as to how that music is to be interacted with, replicated, or performed. Playing various styles of music as background music is another way in which children, parents, and/or carers can be made to feel visible and catered for. While certain music, due to its harmonic, lyrical, or rhythmic complexity, may not be good choices to teach with, that doesn't mean that this music cannot contribute to the rich tapestry of sound in a setting in other ways. Creating inclusive and diverse playlists is a way to not only create inclusive environments but also ensure that music created by Black musicians, members from the LGBTQIA2S+ or East Asian communities is not only played during Black History Month, LGBTQIA2S+ month, or Lunar New Year celebrations. Forming good relationships with caregivers and members of various communities can help educators to make culturally sensitive choices when selecting music for religious or cultural celebrations.

In order to provide an equitable music education in the early years, educators must consider their own positionalities and the history of Whiteness to cater to the most marginalised in their setting. In preparing young children for life in our global society, care must be taken to ensure that children are presented with music that is in equal measure familiar, culturally sensitive, diverse, and helps them develop their own sense of identity. It is up to individual educators to liaise with caregivers to understand the musical environment of each child, and curate settings which create familiarity and yet leave room for inquiry and exploration. In so doing, music education can assist in minimising the effect of Whiteness and contribute to more equitable settings for all.

Notes

1 Identity is made up of more than race, but this will be the focus for this chapter.
2 The term 'Global South' is often used to describe regions of the world that have similar socioeconomic and political statuses, often as a result of European colonialism beginning in the 16th century. These regions include Africa, the Caribbean, Asia, South America, and the Pacific Islands (with some exceptions).
3 The term 'Global North' has also been called the 'Western World', which groups certain regions and countries such as North America, Europe, Australia, Japan, and Singapore according to their socioeconomic and political status.

References

Consortium of National Arts Education Associations. (1994) *National Standards for Arts Education: What Every Young American Should Know and be Able to do in the Arts*. Reston: MENC.

Department for Education (2021) *Survey of Childcare and Early Year Providers: Main Summary, England, 2021*. Available at: https://www.gov.uk/government/statistics/childcare-and-early-years-providers-survey-2021

Dixon, B. (1977) *Catching Them Young*. London: Pluto Press.

Drummond, J. (2005) 'Cultural Diversity in Music Education: Why Bother?'. In P. Shehan Campbell, J. Drummond, P. Dunbar-Hall, K. Howard, H. Schippers and T. Wiggins (eds.), *Cultural Diversity in Music Education*. Brisbane: Australian Academic Press.

Drummond, J. (2008) 'Cultural Diversity in Music Education: Why Bother?'. In P. S. Campbell *et al.* (eds.), *Cultural Diversity in Music Education: Directions and Challenges for the 21st Century*. Austria: Australian Academic Press.

Esquivel, A., Lewis, K., Rodriquex, D. Stovall, D. and Williams, T. (2002) 'We Know What's Best for You: Silencing of People of Colour'. *Counterpoints*, 209, pp. 207–219. Available at: http://www.jstor.org/stable/42979498.

Fields, A. (2020) 'Al, I Wrote the Song, and Directed the Clip in 2014 (Which Was Meant as a Celebration). It Was Not My Intention to Be Culturally Insensitive to the Indian Community, or to Add Value to Ethnic Stereotyping'. *Apologies* [Twitter], 22 October. Available at: https://twitter.com/Anthony_Wiggle/status/1319213117247684609?ref_src=twsrc%5Etfw%7Ctwcamp%5Etweetembed%7Ctwterm%5E1319213117247684609%7Ctwgr%5E%7Ctwcon%5Es1_&ref_url=https%3A%2F%2Fmetro.co.uk%2F2020%2F10%2F24%2Fthe-wiggles-anthony-field-apologises-for-culturally-insensitive-pappadum-song-as-video-goes-viral-13474700%2F.

Freire, P. (1970) *Pedagogy of the Oppressed*. New York: Herder and Herder.

Holder, N. (2020) 'White Violence vs Hip-Hop'. *#DecoloniseMusicEd*. Available at: https://www.nateholdermusic.com/post/white-violence-vs-hip-hop.

Ladson-Billings, G. (1995) 'Toward a Theory of Culturally Relevant Pedagogy'. *American Educational Research Journal*, 32(3), pp. 465–491. Available at: https://doi.org/10.2307/1163320.

Rauscher, F., Shaw, G. and Ky, C. (1993) 'Music and Spatial Task Performance'. *Nature*, 365(611). Available at: https://www.nature.com/articles/365611a0.

Small, C. (1998). *Musicking: The Meanings of Performing and Listening*. Middletown, CT: Wesleyan University Press.

Takacs, D. (2003) 'How Does Your Positionality Bias Your Epistemology?'. *Thought & Action*, 27. Available at: https://repository.uchastings.edu/faculty_scholarship/1264.

Urbach, M. (2019) 'You Might Be Left with Silence When You're Done'; The White Fear of Taking Racist Songs Out of Music Education'. *Medium*. Available at: https://medium.com/@martinurbach/you-might-be-left-with-silence-when-youre-done-the-white-fear-of-taking-racist-songs-out-of-89ecdc300ee5.

Welch, G.F. (2021) 'The Challenge of Ensuring Effective Early Years Music Education by Non-Specialists'. *Early Child Development and Care*, 191(12), pp. 1972–1984.

Part 3
Handling difficult conversations

7
Breaking the last taboo
Talking about Race
Stella Louis and Hannah Betteridge

Having conversations about race can be daunting. Often, it can feel easier to turn a blind eye when we see or hear something troubling than tackle the issue head-on. This could be because we don't have the energy to have a tricky conversation, because we're worried about how the other person might react, or because we're scared of saying the wrong thing and causing offence. If you have ever found yourself in one of these situations, don't worry. They are totally normal and valid fears to have. But, as with most things in life, we must not let our fear of speaking out get in the way when we see or hear someone behaving in a harmful way. No matter how difficult it may feel, having conversations about race is crucial. It is through these discussions that we make progress: we improve understanding, generate empathy, and create environments where people truly feel valued and able to thrive.

It is likely that you will come across a range of different situations pertaining to race, prejudice and discrimination in your day-to-day life that will require a response. Choosing to stay silent in these moments can be extremely damaging for all involved. Not only does silence legitimise racist behaviour by normalising it, but it can also cause 'secondary injury [to the victim that is] akin to rubbing toxins in an open wound' (Kinouani, 2021: 60). Inaction is therefore not a neutral choice. The only thing that silence protects is a system that perpetuates oppression.

But where do I start?

Whether you need to have a difficult conversation with a child, their parent and/or carer, or even one of your colleagues, your starting point should always be the same: yourself. As behavioural scientist, Dr Pragya Agarwal, and entrepreneur, Freddie Harrel, argue, it is important that you have the

DOI: 10.4324/9781003251149-10

difficult conversations about race with yourself first before attempting to have them with anyone else (2019).

It is perhaps unsurprising then that self-reflection is often seen as one of the critical components of anti-racist practice. To develop the tools necessary to talk about race in a constructive, culturally informed, and age-appropriate way, we need to prioritise making the time and space to address our own fears and discomfort. By curating a greater understanding of how we might feel in certain situations, we can stop ourselves projecting our own feelings and/or bias onto situations and instead be fully present in the discussion as it unfolds.

Exercise

Take a moment to find a comfortable spot, grab a notebook and pen, and consider the questions set out below. Some of your answers or the feelings that these questions evoke may surprise you; they may be confronting or triggering. If so, try to avoid judging yourself and, where possible, lean into any feelings of discomfort asking yourself why you feel that way. We encourage you to take a break at any point if you need to and come back when you are ready.

- When and why did you first become aware of your race?
- How has your race affected your life experiences?
- Has anyone ever made you feel inferior for something that you cannot change, such as your skin colour, sexuality, culture, or background? How did you and those around you react? Is there anything you wish you or others had done differently?
- Looking back over the past 12 months, have you proactively created an environment where it feels safe for children, parents and/or carers, or your colleagues to discuss race, prejudice, and discrimination? If so, how have you done this? Is there anything you could do to build on this further?
- Do you find it easy to talk about race without getting defensive? Do you find yourself thinking or saying things that could dismiss another person's feelings or pre-emptively shut down a conversation, such as 'But I would never do that', 'I've struggled in my life, so I don't have privilege', 'I'm not racist, I have Black friends'?

- Do you find yourself looking to your Black and Brown colleagues, friends, and/or family members for answers to questions about how you should tackle race, prejudice, and discrimination?
- Do you look for opportunities to expand the racial diversity of your friendship group or to increase your knowledge and understanding of different cultures? (Sojourner, n.d.)
- Is there anything holding you back from having conversations about race? For each barrier you identify, consider what strategies you could put in place to overcome them.

Make a note of the areas that you would like to work on and revisit this list regularly to inform your continual professional development. Remember, we are all a work in progress and there are always things we wish we had done differently. The important thing is to keep going whilst being kind to ourselves and others.

In this chapter, we will consider the practical steps you can take to create a safe and open space to create a meaningful dialogue with children, their families, and your colleagues in turn. To support you in your journey to becoming an anti-racist educator, your setting should have clear policies and procedures for dealing with racist incidents, as well as clear packages of support if you are personally affected by an incident given the significant levels of trauma that can be evoked. You might find it helpful to familiarise yourself with these policies or have a copy to hand as you work your way through this chapter.

How should I deal with racism in my setting?

In *Talking to Children About Race: Your Guide for Raising Anti-Racist Kids* (2022), broadcaster Loretta Andrews and educator Ruth Hill provide a helpful four-stage model for managing difficult conversations about race with young children:

inform yourself → open a dialogue → model behaviour → support development

It is easy to see how each stage can be implemented as part of your own pedagogical practice. For example, after reading this book (**informing yourself**), you might seek to **open a dialogue** with the children in your setting using books as a resource to scaffold the conversation. In these conversations you can **model behaviour** by using inclusive language and having positive discussions about difference. Based on your observations, you could then develop targeted activities tailored to the unique needs of the child to further **support** their personal, social, and emotional **development.**

However, whilst this model is an incredibly powerful starting point, it is important to note that the process will not always be this linear and the job of an anti-racist educator is an on-going one, with no clear end point. To fully support children to see the beauty in both themselves and others, we need a multitude of tools at our disposal: arguably more so than Andrews and Hill's model suggests. The need for consistent self-reflection, sensitive intervention, and the creation and maintenance of psychological safety are all key components for effective conversations about race which are notably absent from Andrews and Hill's (2022) model. To address these gaps, we have developed a revised framework which seeks to build on the principles that Andrews and Hill (2022) identified (Figure 7.1).

The lateral and non-sequential design of our model seeks to illustrate the interdependencies between each pillar. In doing so, our aim is to encourage practitioners to consider a problem from a range of viewpoints, using

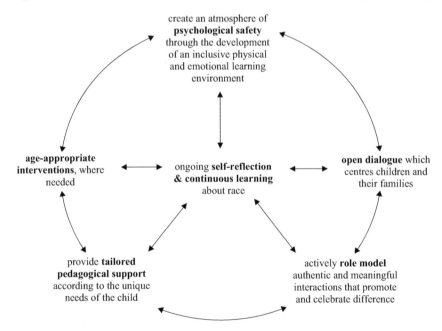

Figure 7.1   Six Pillars to Having Effective Conversations with Children about Race

the multitude of tools at your disposal, whilst firmly embedding the central tenets of anti-racist pedagogy within your practice. Adopting a one size fits all approach to discussions about race is rarely a conducive way to create a meaningful or effective dialogue. To properly support children's development, practitioners need to be able to draw on different techniques, reflecting on what has worked well and what could have gone better as they go. Remember, every child's starting point and the experiences that they bring with them will be different; each child deserves a tailored approach that centres both their voice and their needs.

Open dialogue which centres children and their families from the start

If we start conversations with children and their families at the point that an incident has occurred, we will always be at a disadvantage. We're unlikely to know what children have been exposed to at home or the views of their parents and/or carers. Similarly, their parents and/or carers are unlikely to be aware of the values and/or approach of your setting. Without access to this information, we cannot be properly equipped to navigate potentially emotionally challenging discussions effectively. By setting clear boundaries about what is and is not acceptable early and proactively giving children the tools to discuss racial and cultural differences sensitively, we create a stable foundation for meaningful discussions that children can understand and that families are more willing to partake in. In doing so, we also have the potential to stop racist incidents before they even occur.

As we have emphasised throughout this book, it is never too early to start having conversations about race. Children are naturally curious; at a young age they learn to identify racial, physical, and cultural differences and they will look to us for cues about how to respond in different situations. By age two, you will notice that children in your setting begin talking about how they and others look – skin colour, hair type, eye colour, height, gender, and size become regular topics of conversation. By age three, children begin to comment on 'cultural characteristics that are readily observable, such as language and dress. Many of their comments are in the form of matter-of-fact observations' (Derman-Sparks et al., n.d.: 7). Some children may also already be showing signs that they have assigned negative values to certain physical characteristics through their play and interactions with others.

141

You might hear the following comments or questions:

- 'Why am I White?'
- 'Will you always be Black?'
- 'Will Lola's colour wash off in the bath?'
- 'I have brown eyes. You have blue eyes'.
- 'Your [skin, hair, nose, eyes, mouth] is different to mine'.
- 'Mummy says my skin is caramel'.

It is important that we do not shut down these questions or statements. Whilst they may make us feel uncomfortable or embarrassed, particularly when they point out difference, they do not come from a place intolerance; children are simply learning to navigate the world around them and are working out what these differences mean. Too often educators close down conversations by pretending that they have not heard what a child has said, asking a child to be quiet, or rapidly changing the topic of discussion. When we do this, we teach children that there is something shameful or taboo about race. Instead, we should seek to be open and honest in our communication, using age-appropriate information to respond. For example, you could say: 'Everyone is different. Some people have White skin, some people have Black skin, and some people have brown skin – all of which are beautiful'. Depending on the point raised, you might also find it helpful to unpack what a child has said further by asking open questions, such as 'What makes you say that?'. Whatever the scenario, you should be curious, listen carefully to what the child is saying, and embrace inclusion in your response through both your tone and your words.

Case study – digging beneath the surface

Four-year-old Kendrick is Black and attends a nursery in a predominantly White town in Caerphilly, Wales. During an outdoor activity, Kendrick told Whitney, a White educator, that he only wanted to play with children that were the same colour as him. Although Whitney was uncomfortable responding, she leant into her discomfort and invited him to talk openly about race. Staying focused on the matter at hand, Whitney facilitated a conversation with Kendrick about why it is unfair to treat another child differently because of their race. She highlighted the importance of accepting everyone for who they are and pointed out that even though we may look different to someone else, there is still a lot that connects us.

In response, Kendrick nodded and was silent for a moment before turning to Whitney. 'But James and Sam said they don't play with boys like me! They laughed at my hair', he said. Kendrick had Afro-textured hair which had been recently braided into cornrows. By staying curious and actively listening to what Kendrick was saying, Whitney realised that his earlier statement about wanting to play with children that looked like him could have been a self-protection mechanism. She sat with him and spoke to him about how James and Sam's approach made him feel, whilst re-affirming his cultural and racial identity, telling him how beautiful his hair was. She also talked through some strategies to help him respond to inappropriate statements that were either directed at him or others, and ended the conversation by reiterating that she was always here if he wanted to talk or needed support in a situation.

Over the next few weeks and months, Whitney made a concerted effort to improve the representation of Black men and women across the nursery through different activities to normalise Black culture. She also carved out time to speak to James and Sam to counter their views by exposing them to difference in a positive way and encouraging empathy.

Whitney's approach was rooted in asking open questions without judgement. This allowed Kendrick to lead the conversation and created an environment where he could fully express how he was feeling without judgement. Had she shut down the conversation or just told him off for saying he did not want to play with children that were of a different to race to him, it is unlikely that she would have identified the wider issue at hand.

For discussions with children's parents and/or carers, we strongly recommend that practitioners consider how they can raise awareness of and promote the anti-racist values of their setting from day one. Initial meetings with parents and inductions are a fantastic opportunity to discuss what being an anti-racist nursery means to you, how you will raise any issues of concerns, and discuss how learning can be extended at home or in the nursery. You could also invite all parents to participate in a family tree exercise, bringing in photos of family members that can be displayed in the setting, or ask them to complete an exercise with their children designed to support children to express who they are and build pride in their own identity. Some parents and/ or carers will react positively, perhaps talking about what they do at home to support their child's learning or what cultural traditions are particularly important to them. Others may speak positively about the approach, but not wish to take part. And some may find these discussions confronting or in direct opposition to their own values. Going into these discussions, it is important to be prepared to handle questions such as:

- 'Children are colour-blind. Aren't we just feeding racism by focusing on it all the time?'
- 'I don't want you to talk to my child my race and racism. They're too young to understand! Kids should just be kids'.

In these scenarios, we have found that factual answers work best. For example, you might want to highlight some of the studies we have shared in this book which demonstrate that children not only see race from a young age, but internalise beliefs based on societal norms that can be detrimental to their sense of self or others (Goodman, 1952; Clark and Clark, 1947). Reassure them that your intention is not to make children of the majority group feel guilty about their race; it is to prepare the children in your setting to be compassionate citizens of the world.

The importance of psychological safety

Discussing race is not just difficult for us; it can also be difficult for children, their families, and our colleagues. As educators we have a choice: we can create an inclusive environment where psychological safety is paramount, or we can create a hostile environment where people are too scared to ask questions and say how they feel. This is not always a conscious decision. Our silence and inaction, borne out of fear or embarrassment, still teaches children that their racial and cultural identity is not valued and that there is something inherently taboo about discussing race, even if that is not our intention.

> **Psychological safety** in this context is used to describe a feeling that it is safe to express your thoughts or concerns or ask for help. It is the knowledge that you will not be judged or humiliated for making mistakes or labelled as a troublemaker when you surface issues about race.

The importance of establishing psychological safety when discussing race in early years settings is a relatively unexplored area of study. In the process of researching this book, we found very limited data on: (a) the extent to which children, their families, or educators feel emotionally safe addressing issues about race, and (b) the impact that an absence of psychological safety can have on someone's mental health and wellbeing. However, based on our own experience of discussing race with parents and educators, we have heard countless stories from people who have said that they have been too scared to challenge examples of racism or prejudice because of a fear of that it could make matters for them or their children worse. Instead, they typically tend to leave their jobs, find new arrangements for their children, or suffer in silence at a great personal cost to their emotional wellbeing. For children, who may not yet have the words to articulate the impact that certain situations or discussions have had on them, we believe the absence of psychological safety can have a particularly profound effect on their growing sense of self. It can lead them to despise themselves, hide parts of who they are, and feel inferior (see Chapter 3 for more information on racial trauma).

Despite the lack of academic attention it has received to date, psychological safety in early years settings matters. After all, nobody can truly thrive in an environment where they do not feel safe. When we create open spaces for learning we can better support children to understand difference and empower them to stand up for what is right. In our experience, this starts by:

- Proactively giving children the language to express themselves – their thoughts, feelings, and fears – to create favourable conditions for learning where children feel comfortable expressing, sharing, and asking questions.
- Being mindful of our tone and body language.
- Giving factual answers to difficult questions.
- Reassuring children that it is not just ok to be different from those around us, but that difference is a positive thing.
- Validating the feelings of the injured party by acknowledging the impact the situation or action has had on them. This includes not making excuses that can belittle or diminish someone's experience by making them feel as though the issue lies with them being too sensitive rather than with the problematic behaviour or action (e.g., 'I know you are upset, but I'm sure they didn't mean it that way').
- Receive feedback gracefully and take strategic action to address racist or prejudicial behaviour in a timely way.

- See mistakes as a learning opportunity. Instead of reacting angrily and punishing children when they do something wrong, we can use these moments as a chance to expand their understanding of others and build empathy.

Be a role model

As an educator, you are in a uniquely powerful position to support children to embrace and celebrate difference as part of the beauty of life. The children in your setting will constantly be observing not just your words and actions, but your tone and body language. They absorb these cues and use them to make sense of the world around them. As Alicia Sojourner, an equity and inclusion specialist based in Vancouver, points out, '[e]ven the smallest actions can sometimes send negative signals to a child' (n.d.). She encourages practitioners to think about their own actions asking whether you tend to sit near people of your own race in public, or whether you smile when someone makes an ethnic joke even if it makes you feel uncomfortable to avoid confrontation (Sojourner, n.d.) Taking this one step further, we would encourage you to think about not just who you may choose to sit next to, but who you tend to gravitate towards the most in your settings and what messages this may send to the other children and staff.

If you want to support the children in your setting to adopt an anti-racist mindset, you need to demonstrate how you live these values yourself. You can search out new and diverse educational materials, immerse yourself in different cultures to enrich your understanding of other people's cultures, provide space for other people to tell their stories, learn words and phrases in different languages that the children in your setting speak, or plan trips that can help a child see life from a different perspective. The opportunities are endless.

Knowing how and when to intervene

In the field of child development, we often talk about the importance of 'child-led play' and 'child-led learning'. Under both approaches, educators have a key role to play, which includes knowing when to stand back and let children work things out for themselves, versus when we need to step in and provide support or guidance.

'**Child-led play**' and '**child-led learning**' (sometimes referred to as independent learning or child-initiated activities) are based on the principle that children should be given opportunities to make free and active choices about what they would like to do, with educators playing a supporting role focused on allowing children to learn at their own pace and pursue activities that are naturally of interest to them, rather than directing children to a desired activity. Effective learning environments promote a mixture of both child and adult led activity.

Across all areas of our practice, we should seek to embed positive ways of working with children that enable us to be responsive to their needs and interests, allowing them to expand their knowledge and understanding of the world organically, with sensitive interventions where needed. Yet, when it comes to race, we have heard time and time again that the fear of getting it wrong can inhibit educators from intervening, even when they know they should. In the same way you wouldn't hesitate to intervene if a child was about to come to physical harm, you shouldn't question intervening if you can see that a child is about to come to emotional harm or inflict emotional harm onto others. However, care should be given to how and when you intervene. As a general rule, your intervention should be timely, sensitive, age-appropriate, and address the issue at hand directly with all of the children involved and, where appropriate, their families.

It is not enough just to say 'we don't say that' or 'that's wrong'. For children to truly learn the impact of their actions, they need to understand why. Weaving in your knowledge and understanding of child development at this point is crucial; you need to know how able and willing a child is to consider the situation from someone else's point of view and adapt your approach accordingly. For example, if we accept Piaget's assertion that the brain development of young children is often characterised by egocentrism, we know that children 'believe that other people see, hear and feel the same as them, and they can find it difficult to understand that people have different perspectives on the same situation' as a result (Piaget, 1955; Agarwal, 2020: 58). Therefore, in a situation where a young child has said or done something problematic, it follows logically that our intervention will be more effective if we first ask them to consider how they would feel if X had happened to them rather than just saying 'that upset Anisha' because the latter doesn't enable them to understand why.

Yvonne Conolly, Britain's first Black primary school headteacher, set out several principles for working with young children, which we believe also provide a solid foundation for helping educators decide when an intervention is necessary. Connolly (as quoted in Bruce, 1987: 149) asserted that:

- 'Children need a sense of belonging.
- Children must not be placed in a dilemma about their own sense of worth.
- People must be allowed to identify themselves, and others should not do it for them.
- [T]he natural "stranger fear" of people needs to be overcome through positive strategies of action'.

Using these principles as a guide, it is our view that any situation which impacts negatively on a child's sense of belonging, self-worth, ability to define themselves or promotes a fear or distrust of a different racial group necessitate that an educator should take action to protect and promote their individual needs.

Equally, it is important to know when not to intervene too. For example, if we were to observe two children from different racial backgrounds arguing over blocks, it would be wrong for us to assume that race was the driving factor behind this interaction and intervene by discussing racism with each of the children. Instead, we need to use our observations to fully assess the situation before making a judgement call about whether to step in. In some circumstances, it may be beneficial to give children the space to work things out for themselves – e.g., if what we are seeing is just a quick squabble between two children the likelihood is that they can probably resolve it nicely on their own and in providing them the space to do so we are supporting the development of their problem-solving skills. In others, some form of intervention may be needed but we still need to guard against assuming that an intervention on the grounds of race is necessary – e.g., if the situation starts to escalate with one child grabbing or shoving another, it might be necessary to separate the two children and have a discussion about sharing. Adapting our approach according to the situation and giving children the space to explain the drivers behind their behaviour without jumping to conclusions is crucial.

Tailored support that meets the unique needs of the child

Identity development in young children is complex due to the overlapping effects of race, social class, gender, ethnicity, culture, and disability – all of which contribute towards who they are. Whilst a child may be outwardly perceived as belonging to a specific social category, their self-perception may vary and evolve over time (Siraj-Blatchford and Clarke, 2000). We must avoid projecting our own personal views of child's identity (who we think they are or should be) onto them. Instead, we should be led by them and their families, providing space for their voices in our practice. At best, in failing to provide this means we disregard the uniqueness of the child. At worst, we can create an internal schism within a child's developing sense of self as they consider how they relate to others and decide who they are.

Personal reflection

Growing up mixed-race, I (Hannah) was frequently told by teachers, children, and other adults what I was and how I should define myself. Some would tell me matter-of-factly that I was Black and others would joke that I was a 'coconut' or a 'Bounty' – Black on the outside but White on the inside. Neither of these resonated with how I saw myself and I spent a lot of my childhood confused. As a young child I would look at my mum, who is Black, and my dad, who is White, and I could clearly see that my skin was different to both of theirs. In being told I was Black, I felt like I was being asked to ignore my dad, his family, and the cultural traditions I learned from them. I also felt incredibly guilty and ashamed for not internally identifying as Black when others were telling me that I was.

It was only as I grew older and reached my late teens that I realised I didn't need to be Black or White; that being mixed-race was a racial identity in and of itself. I didn't need to tear myself in two and stake a claim or one or the other. After years of being at war with myself, I could just be me.

When we put children into a box of our making, the impact can be significant. Without them even realising it, the judgements and labels that others placed on me interfered with my own sense of self and personal, social, and emotional development whilst I was growing up. It caused a lot of unnecessary turmoil that could have been avoided if only I had been asked how I saw myself or someone had spoken to my parents about the mix of cultural traditions we embraced at home, rather than making assumptions about where I best fit.

This is not just an issue for mixed-race children. Educators should never assume that all children from a particular community or racial group are a homogenous group with a shared set of experiences, or that their self-perceptions are the same. Just as there is a lot of variety in how a White person from London or New York might identify themselves based on which part of the city they grew up in or the impact of other factors (e.g., their religion, socio-economic background, or gender), a Black Caribbean child of St Lucian heritage may identify differently from a Black Caribbean child of Jamaican heritage, despite both being Black and from the Caribbean. In building genuine partnerships with the children in our care and their families, we are better able to understand all the component parts of a child's identity and how they combine together to make them whole.

As we've spoken about elsewhere in the book, tailoring the support we provide to meet the unique needs of the child necessitates that we:

- Recognise and tackle our own unconscious bias – if we don't, we risk limiting the learning opportunities we offer to children and make false assumptions about what they need or would benefit from. (See Chapter 2 for more information on unravelling bias.)
- Make space for the voice of the child so that we can accurately assess where they are at, what they need and plan accordingly. (See Chapter 3 for more practical guidance on how to do this within your own practice.)
- Build an inclusive learning environment that supports children of all races to feel like they belong and are valued. (See Chapters 4, 5, and 6 for further details on how to embed diversity and inclusion within the physicality of your setting and in the activities you design.)

However, the toolbox that we draw from to support a White child or a child from an ethnic minority background to understand race, prejudice, and discrimination will often be different. For the former, our task as educators typically tends to be designed around supporting them to become anti-racist citizens, whereas for the latter our role is often to support them to thrive in spite of the system of oppression that surrounds them.

Studies have proven that a child's positive-esteem heavily depends upon whether the child feels that others accept them and see them as competent and worthwhile (Manning-Morton and Thorp, 2003). For children from an ethnic minority background, this can be harder to establish particularly when they begin to comprehend that being White is favoured more highly (Derman-Sparks and Edwards, 2010). In these scenarios, we need to tailor our approach and design interventions that seek to increase a child's self-esteem and pride in themselves.

 ## Case study – a woman like me

In one setting, we observed a little girl speaking to her keyworker about how much she disliked her Afro hair. The educator worked with her to see the positives in her curly, bouncy hair. They made sure that there were books and images in the setting that reflected what the child looked like and their family. They talked to her parents about hair care so they could improve their own understanding and build this into the conversations they were having. Further opportunities for learning were also created by inviting a Black female doctor to talk to the children about their job. In seeing a successful woman with similar hair, the educator was successfully able to counter some of the negative messages that the little girl had previously absorbed about herself; namely, that success only came with Eurocentric features.

For White children, the approach we take may be different but requires no less thought. In helping White children to construct an accurate view of the world we need to strike the right balance between providing windows into other realities and experiences and supporting them to understand what it means to be White without creating or perpetuating feelings of shame or guilt. As Abraham F Citron explains:

> As white child grows, he gradually assumes an unconscious feeling of white dominance. He orients himself in a white-centric world. The white self is felt as the human norm, the right, against which all persons of color may be judged.

> (1969:1)

This creates a distorted perception of reality – one where the White child is ill-equipped to build meaningful social and personal relationships with appreciation or navigate today's world.

As we seek to rebalance this world view through exposure to people of different racial and ethnic backgrounds and activities designed to highlight the value that diversity and inclusion brings, we need to actively challenge the stereotypes and White-centric narratives that they have absorbed. For example, after reading a book or completing an activity about race, we might find it helpful to explain that for a long time people weren't treated equally based on the colour of their skin and the impact that this has had using examples that children can relate to, like who was allowed to go to school. In doing so, we can describe how the legacy of these systems can still be seen today which disproportionately benefits White people, whilst still being clear that this is not the child's fault, it is just incumbent on all of us to change it.

On-going self-reflection and continuous learning

The good news is attitudes and biases are not fixed. They can change, grow, develop, and reduce as we learn new information and expose ourselves to different perspectives. Participating in unconscious bias training or reading books like this one can provide a solid foundation for raising awareness of how our attitudes affect our behaviour both consciously and unconsciously. However, no stand-alone training, book, article, or podcast can successfully dismantle a lifetime of exposure to stereotypes, prejudice, or discrimination. Being aware of your bias is only the first step.

To improve outcomes, educators need to go further. We need to put systems and strategies in place that allow us to embed behaviour change into our pedagogical practice at an individual level and work with our employers to ensure equity, diversity and inclusion are ingrained into the DNA of our settings at an organisational level. This requires continuous thought, reflection, and action. We have peppered examples of how you can do this throughout this book from keeping a reflective journal to embedding group supervision into your practice and building regular space for courageous conversations about race into team meetings and continuous professional development days.

Further reading on how to have discussions with children about race

Talking to children about race can feel like a minefield. Thankfully, in the last few years a range of resources have been developed to support and empower you to have positive and constructive discussions about race. This list is not exhaustive, but we hope it will be helpful should you need any further information or guidance.

- Dr Pragya Agarwal's *Wish We Knew What to Say: Talking with Children about Race*. London. Dialogue Books.
- Freddie Harrel and Dr Pragya Agarwal for Women's Hour, 'How to Talk to Your Children about Race and Racism'. Available at: https://www.bbc.co.uk/programmes/articles/7xvLw6Q4qbJBnkz kj6xm9Z/how-to-talk-to-your-children-about-race-and-racism.
- Laura Henry-Allain MBE and Matt Lloyd-Rose's online resource 'The Tiney Guide to Becoming an Inclusive, Anti-Racist Early Educator'. Available at: https://www.tiney.co/blog/becoming-an-inclusive-anti-racist-early-educator/.
- Liz Pemberton's guide to 'Managing the Reporting of a Racist Incident Between Children'. Available via www.thatnurserylife. com.
- NSPCC's online guide for 'Talking to Children About Racism'. Available at: https://www.nspcc.org.uk/keeping-children-safe/ support-for-parents/children-race-racism-racial-bullying/.
- Uju Asika's *Bringing Up Race: How to Raise a Kind Child in a Prejudiced World*. London. Yellow Kite.

Having difficult conversations with staff

In order to have difficult conversations about race and discrimination, it is paramount that all educators within a setting understand why conversing about issues of race is important and feel confident doing so. This means facilitating conversations with your colleagues to find out how they feel about their own racial identity and that of others. This will not only help to break down barriers and normalise discussions about race but will also improve the opportunities offered to individual children in your setting.

Case study – mirror, mirror

In a small nursery in South East London, a team of educators were encouraged to look at representation in their setting, with a focus on who was represented and who was not and which representations were positive and which were not. Each of the educators took turns sharing their reflections with the group. Pamela, a White educator, said: 'Does it really matter? Kids from different backgrounds can just look in the mirror if they want to see themselves represented!'

In the discussion that followed, Pamela's comments (rather than Pamela as a person) were constructively challenged by the other educators and facilitator. Pamela was encouraged to reflect on how her attitude played out in practice and whether or not that approach disproportionately benefitted one race over others. Her colleagues asked open questions, such as 'why do you feel that is sufficient?' and 'what evidence do you have to support that view?', and encouraged her to consider what it would be like to not see yourself represented in the world around you, or to only see yourself represented in unfavourable terms.

During this process, individual participants paid as much attention to their tone and body language as they did to their words. All too often in these scenarios we see personal attacks levied at an individual, with comments like 'you're so ignorant', or hostile body language, including eye rolling, which tends to put people in defensive mode rather than listening mode. By developing and following a clear set of rules at the start of the session that was designed to ensure the discussion was a truly safe space, participants were able to help Pamela reflect on what she has just said through an honest dialogue about racial representation.

At the end of the session Pamela openly reflected on how unaware she was of the extent to which she had benefitted from Whiteness being presented as the default throughout her life. She acknowledged that she had never had to question whether she belonged in a space and how the absence of these questions had blinded her to the alternative.

We all have a role to play in creating safe spaces where both us as individuals and our colleagues are encouraged to push past any fears and feelings of discomfort to talk openly and honestly about race. If we shroud these conversations in judgement and shame, people will naturally be less willing to engage in the future which ultimately prevent us from making progress.

That doesn't mean we need to give colleagues a free pass to say things that are racist; instead, it's about finding constructive ways to challenge problematic words and behaviour. As a group and as individuals, we need to have strategies in place to address and deal with avoidance or inappropriate conversations; be able to support our colleagues to acknowledge and or manage their own feelings, attitudes, and behaviours; and be aware that sometimes individuals (including ourselves) may require additional support after the conversation has ended.

Some educators may avoid openly discussing race which can put children at a disadvantage.

 # Case study – opposing views

Carol is White and a firm believer in 'colour blindness'. She is the keyworker for three-year-old Nana, who is Black. In her assessments, Carol assessed Nana as lagging behind with her communication skills. When Nana's communication style was discussed in the team meeting, Jomoke, a Black educator from South Africa, shared her observations communicating and interacting with Nana. After some discussion amongst the others, Jomoke suggested that maybe Carol had not understood what Nana had been saying because her accent was unfamiliar, and she had mistakenly under assessed her because of the way that she pronounces some of her words. Carol became visibly upset, stating that when she assesses children she does not see their colour, she sees all children as the same. Carol said that Jomoke had made her feel like she was a racist and refused to discuss the matter further.

To take the heat out the situation, Rob, the nursery manager, suggested the group take a five-minute break before reconvening. When they returned, he acknowledged Carol's fears and how she was feeling. However, he was clear that a child's race, accent, and cultural heritage must be considered as part of the whole child assessment and noted the importance of continuing the discussion and considering Jomoke's perspectives to ensure they could provide Nana with the right support.

Rob facilitated the rest of the discussion, assigning time to focus on the aspects of Nana's communication skills where there was agreement within the team and encouraged all to listen, reflect and to embrace this as a learning opportunity. At the end of the discussion Carol was keen to go away and observe Nana again. When the team met again two weeks later Carol reported that she been misguided in her initial assessment. After paying more attention to not just watching but listening actively to Nana, she was able to see how much Nana communicates with the other children and staff in the setting. Carole also said that in making more space to listen to Nana she had developed a better sense of her interests and learning preferences. Taking part in the discussion rather that cutting it short allowed for a more holistic assessment of where Nana was at and ensured that she was supported effectively.

This is not an uncommon experience. According to the Southern Poverty Law Center's 'Learning for Justice' project, when educators become concerned about coming across as racist, they may avoid talking about race on any level because the fear of looking or being perceived to be racist consumes them (Blackburn *et al.*, 2022). This can create a hostile environment by putting other educators off from asking questions and ultimately lead to poorer outcomes for the children in our care.

Interpreting young children's learning and development is a complex task. One way to ensure that assessments are free of bias is to ask two colleagues who do not work directly with the child in question to look at and interpret the same observations independent of the other so that they do not know what the other persons opinion is (Louis, 2020). Once the observations have been completed and written down, the two should be compared and discussed with the observers asked to point to evidence to justify their conclusions. Comparing notes will help you identify and recognise bias in your thinking as you detangle the actual observation – what happened verses your perception of what happened – and provides a useful bank of evidence from which to start or continue a discussion.

Although sometimes challenging, these discussions encourage educators to pay careful attention to their inner thoughts and behaviours, helping us to identify any implicit assumptions that we may hold. Regular exposure to other points of view also enables us to challenge stereotypes and question deeply rooted beliefs about children and families from a different racial groups to ourselves.

Reflective questions

It is only by questioning our own beliefs and asking tough questions that we can truly take into account the impact that our own identity and background can have on our pedagogical practice and the way we make young children feel about themselves. Ask yourself:

- In the last three months, have you asked yourself and other educators tough questions in order to challenge unconscious bias and stereotypes?
- How are you supporting your colleagues to think about whether the learning opportunities they are providing are narrowing or supporting children's learning experience?
- How do you make these conversations feel safe, so that you and your colleagues can be honest with yourselves and others no matter how uncomfortable the topic is?

For your Black and Brown colleagues and the children of colour in your care, silence will never be a luxury that is afforded to them. In every room they enter, they cannot be silent, their skin won't let them; it speaks on their behalf (Boakye, 2022). Avoiding the difficult conversations or dismissing problematic behaviour as 'kids just being kids' has real consequences for all involved. It allows racism, prejudice, and discrimination to thrive in our settings and can be hugely damaging for children from ethnic minority backgrounds, their families and our staff. It is incumbent upon all of us to proactively create safe spaces where children and staff feel empowered to celebrate difference and stand up for what is right.

Further reading to continue learning about race

The journey to becoming an anti-racist educator is an on-going one. To support you as you continue down this path, we have pulled together a selection of our favourite materials which seek to educate and raise awareness about race. This is by no means an exhaustive list, but we hope it will be a useful starting point if you would like further information or guidance.

- Akala's *Natives: Race and Class in the Ruins of the Empire*. Great Britain: Two Roads.

- Emma Dabiri's *What White People Can Do Next: From Allyship to Coalition*. London: Penguin.
- Louise Derman-Sparks and Carol Phillips' *Teaching/Learning Anti-Racism: A Developmental Approach*. New York: Teachers College Press.
- Louise Derman-Sparks and Patricia Ramsey's *What If All the Kids Are White? Anti-bias Multicultural Education With Young Children And Families*. New York: Teachers College Press.
- Robin DiAngelo's *White Fragility: Why It's So Hard for White People to Talk About Racism*. London: Penguin.
- Reni Eddo-Lodge's *Why I'm No Longer Talking to White People About Race*. London: Bloomsbury.
- Afua Hirsch's *Brit(ish) on Race, Identity and Belonging*. London: Vintage.
- Binna Kandola's *Racism at Work: The Danger of Indifference*. Oxford: Pearn Kandola Publishing.
- Ibram X Kendy's *How to be an Anti-Racist*. London: Penguin.
- Guilaine Kinouani's *Living While Black*. London: Ebury Publishing.
- Ijeoma Oluo's *So You Want to Talk About Race*. New York: Seal Press.

References

Agarwal, P. (2020) *Wish We Knew What to Say: Talking with Children about Race*. London. Dialogue Books.

Andrews, L. and Hill, R. (2022) *Talking to Children About Race: Your Guide for Raising Anti-Racist Kids*. London: SPCK.

Blackburn, S.S., Burkhalter, K., Jones, J. and Wai, C. (2022) *Let's Talk: Facilitating Critical Conversations with Students*. 2nd edn. Washington: The Southern Poverty Law Center.

Boakye, J. (2022) *I Heard What Your Said: A Black Teacher, A White System, A Revolution in Education*. London: Picador.

Bruce, T. (1987) *Early Childhood Education*. London: Hodder and Stoughton.

Citron, A.F. (1969) *The "Rightness of Whiteness": The World of a White Child in a Segregated Society*. Michigan: Michigan-Ohio Regional Educational Laboratory. Available at: https://files.eric.ed.gov/fulltext/ED033261.pdf.

Clark, K.B. and Clark, M.P. (1947) 'Racial Identification and Preference in Negro Children'. In T.M. Newcomb and E.L. Hartley (eds.) *Readings in Social Psychology*. New York: Rinehart & Winston, pp. 602–611.

Derman-Sparks, L. and Olsen Edwards, J. (2010) *Anti-bias Education for Young Children and Ourselves*. Washington: NAEYC.

Derman-Sparks, L., Tanka Higa, C. and Sparks, B. (n.d.) *Children, Race and Racism: How Race Awareness Develops*. Early Childhood Equity Alliance. Available at: https://www.teachingforchange.org/wp-content/uploads/2012/08/ec_children raceracism_english.pdf.

Goodman, M.E. (1952) *Race Awareness in Young Children*. New York: Collier Books.

Harrel, F. and Agarwal, P. (2019) 'Women's Hour: How to Talk to Your Children about Race and Racism'. *BBC* [Radio Programme], 17 August. Available at: https://www .bbc.co.uk/programmes/articles/7xvLw6Q4qbJBnkzkj6xm9Z/how-to-talk-to-your -children-about-race-and-racism.

Kinouani, G. (2021) *Living While Black: The Essential Guide to Overcoming Racial Trauma*. London: Ebury Press.

Louis, S. (2020) *How to use Work Group Supervision to Improve Early Years Practice*. London: Routledge.

Manning-Morton, J. and Thorp, M. (2003) *Key Times for Play: The First Three Years*. Maidenhead: Open University Press.

Piaget, J. (1955) *The Language and Thought of the Child*. London: Routledge and Kegan Paul.

Siraj-Blatchford, I. and Clarke, P. (2000) *Supporting Identity, Diversity and Language in the Early Years*. Bucks: Open University Press.

Sojourner, A. (n.d.) *How to Talk with Kids about Race and Racism*. Schools in Sites. Available at: https://content.schoolinsites.com/api/documents/e44e445a9cfe4ce 6ba709c09c86bad27.pdf

8

Our hope for a brighter future

Hannah Betteridge

On a cold and grey wintery day, we sat in our homes crying over video call. The case study that we had spent the last 30 minutes writing together, following a conversation with an early years practitioner, had triggered a particularly painful flashback from childhood that had lain in wait, dormant for years.

As we looked at each other through the screen, it was all too easy to conjure an image of the child's face in our minds. It was a face we knew too well. The furrowed brow weighed down by confusion and shame. The tear-stained cheeks littered with disappointment. Why? Because another child had experienced what it was like to be treated as less than simply because of the colour of their skin. As our collective hurt hung in the air, we were reminded once again of the immense power that educators have to shape a young child's experiences.

There were many moments like this whilst writing *Let's Talk About Race in the Early Years*. We found the process cathartic at times, triggering at others. Throughout it all, one thing kept us going: hope.

Hope that our children and grandchildren will grow up in a world that values them, sees their beauty, and shines a little brighter for it.

Hope that #BlackGirlMagic and #BlackBoyMagic become more than just Twitter trends.

Hope that one day a world exists where this book is no longer needed.

In the wake of George Floyd's murder, it finally felt like the pendulum had swung towards progress. There was a sense of momentum and urgency for collective action against racism that gave us hope, for the first time in a long time, that things would be different. Yet, just two years later, as we poured ourselves into these pages, we were confronted over and over again with just how much further we still have to go.

First, in March 2022, details were released of a harrowing incident where a 15-year-old Black girl, known as Child Q, was taken out of an exam and

DOI: 10.4324/9781003251149-11

strip-searched in a school medical room by two female police officers whilst on her period, after her teachers called the police over concerns that she had drugs in her possession because she allegedly smelled like cannabis. No other adults were present during the search and her parents were not contacted. No drugs were found. The review into the incident concluded that a search never should have happened and 'that racism (whether deliberate or not) was likely to have been an influencing factor in the decision to undertake a strip search' (City of London and Hackney Safeguarding Children Partnership, 2022: 32). In the outrage that followed, it was revealed that 650 children had been strip-searched in London between 2018 and 2020. Most were innocent of the crimes they had been suspected of. Appropriate adults were often absent. The vast majority were Black (Weale and Dodd, 2022).

Then, in September 2022, moments away from where we both live, Chris Kaba, a 24-year-old unarmed Black man and father, was shot dead by the police whilst driving. Chris Kaba was not suspected of any crime. The police failed to use their lights or sirens whilst they pursued him in an unmarked police car, making it unlikely that he would have known who he was being chased by in his final moments. Whilst investigations are ongoing, Chris's family, friends, and community are left grieving the loss of another innocent Black man brutally killed at the hands of an institution that's mission is to protect us.

For most people of colour, these events were horrifying, yes, but shocking, no. The colour of your skin should not be a death sentence, but in far too many cases it still is. Despite all the signs of progress and the promises of change made in the wake of George Floyd's murder, these events serve as a prominent reminder that racism is still alive and kicking. The work needed to dismantle it is just as vital and urgent as ever. Perhaps if the people and institutions surrounding us were taught not to see Child Q and Chris Kaba's skin colour as a threat, neither of their stories would have ended so tragically.

Without an awareness of this context, we cannot begin to equip the children we teach with the skills they need to navigate the world around them. Often, feelings of guilt and powerlessness can nudge us into silence when we are confronted with such traumatic events, but silence will never drive change. Remember: whilst you cannot control the world around you, you can control the world you create in the educational settings that you work in.

As an educator, you have the power to support every child to love the skin they are born in. You can teach them that there is beauty in difference;

161

that melanin is not their enemy. You can guide them to become responsible, compassionate, and anti-racist citizens of the world.

It will not be easy. At times it may feel impossible, and you won't always get it right. In those moments, dig deep and keep going. Remember that the nature of your role places you in a uniquely powerful position to stop racist attitudes from ever even forming.

Throughout your career, you will play a critical role in creating favourable conditions for the social, emotional, and intellectual development of every child that you teach. Take racial and cultural identity as seriously as literacy and numeracy. Build moments of reflection and challenge into your practice to give you the time and space to consider your attitudes, preconceptions, and your vulnerability to bias. Consider your observations, assessments, and planning procedures to ensure that they are fair and equitable and avoid perpetuating existing racial inequalities. Give young children and their families a voice; make them feel seen, valued, and heard.

Today is the day. Do something. Do more. Do better.

References

City of London and Hackney Safeguarding Children Partnership (2022) *Local Child Safeguarding Practice Review: Child Q.* Available at: https://chscp.org.uk/wp-content/uploads/2022/03/Child-Q-PUBLISHED-14-March-22.pdf.

Weale, S. and Dodd, V. (2022) 'Revealed: Met Police Strip-Searched 650 Children in Two-Year Period'. *The Guardian*, 8 August. Available at: https://www.theguardian.com/uk-news/2022/aug/08/police-data-raises-alarm-over-welfare-of-strip-searched-children.

Index

Printed in the United States
by Baker & Taylor Publisher Services